Aitareya Upaniṣad

Rediscovering Indian Literary Classics

(ISSN - 0972-0111)

1. Taittirīya Upaniṣad: With the Original Text in Sanskrit and Roman Transliteration. Translation with an Exhaustive Commentary; by Muni Narayana Prasad. (ISBN 81-246-0014-7)

2,4-5. Bṛhadāraṇyaka Upaniṣad: With Original Text in Roman Transliteration. English Translation and Appendices; by Nitya Chaitanya Yati; **Vol. 1**: Madhu Kāṇḍa; **Vol. 2**: Muni Kāṇḍa; **Vol. 3**: Khila Kāṇḍa (ISBN 81-246-0008-2)

3. Kena Upaniṣad: With the Original Text in Sanskrit and Roman Transliteration. Translation with an Extensive Commentary; by Muni Narayana Prasad. (ISBN 81-246-0034-1)

6. Muṇḍaka Upaniṣad: With the Original Text in Sanskrit and Roman Transliteration. Translation with an Exhaustive Commentary; by Muni Narayana Prasad. (ISBN 81-246-0105-4)

7. Kaṭha Upaniṣad: With the Original Text in Sanskrit and Roman transliteration. Translation with an Exhaustive Commentary; by Muni Narayana Prasad. (ISBN 81-246-0110-0)

8. Praśna Upaniṣad: With the Original Text in Sanskrit and Roman transliteration. Translation with an Extensive Commentary; by Muni Narayana Prasad. (ISBN 81-246-0129-1)

9. Aitareya Upaniṣad: With the Original Text in Sanskrit and Roman transliteration. Translation with an Extensive Commentary; by Muni Narayana Prasad. (ISBN 81-246-0142-9)

Rediscovering Indian Literary Classics, no. 9

Aitareya Upaniṣad

with the original text in
Sanskrit and Roman transliteration

Translation with
an Extensive Commentary

by

Swami Muni Narayana Prasad

D.K.Printworld(P)Ltd.
NEW DELHI - 110 015

Cataloging in Publication Data — DK

Narayana Prasad, *Muni*, 1938-
Aitareya Upaniṣad.
(Rediscovering Indian literary classics; no. 9).
Includes Index.
ISBN 13: 9788124601426
ISBN 10: 8124601429

1. Upanishads. Aitareyopaniṣad — Commentaries.
2. Hinduism — Sacred books. 3. Philosophy, Hindu.
I. Upanishads. Aitareyopaniṣad. English & Sanskrit. II. Title.
III. Series: Rediscovering Indian literary classics; no. 9.

First Published in India in 2000
Second impression, 2011

ISBN 13: 978-81-246-0142-6 (Pb) ISBN 10: 81-246-0142-9

Printed and published by:
D.K. Printworld (P) Ltd.
Regd. office : *'Srikunj'*, F-52, Bali Nagar
Ramesh Nagar Metro Station
New Delhi – 110 015
Phones : (011) 2545 3975, 2546 6019
Fax : (011) 2546 5926
E-mail : indology@dkprintworld.com
Web : www.dkprintworld.com

Foreword

IT is by the grace of Swami Muni Narayana Prasad, that we, the *Gurukula* inmates, are being initiated into the path of contemplation. I had the fortune to stay with him as a student for 12 years, during which he has been writing commentaries, mainly on the crowning texts of wisdom, the Upaniṣads.

The Upaniṣads are unexpended mines of contemplative spirituality. It is uttered in the moments of ecstacy in mellifluous poetic diction by Indian seers. A seer or a *guru* of that order represents in his person the throb of the Absolute. And the disciple is the recepient who imbibes that living spirit in aweful adoration and gratitude. Such is the context out of which all the Upaniṣads are born.

That which was conveyed in such moments of ecstacy remains as a verbal testimony for mankind to chew and digest. It is also the precious treasure chests to be preserved by mankind for the generations to come.

The Upaniṣads are rendered in archaic Sanskrit language. They are so subtle that almost all of them are very hard nuts to crack. This prompted the continuaters of wisdom-heritage to produce explications, elaborate or brief. Here also we have such a work in hand by Swami Muni Narayana Prasad.

In former days it was for the anterior skeptics that the masters produced their insights in the form of authentic commentories. In the *Gurukula* also there arose a similar demanding situation that gave vent to the birth of present explication.

In each Upaniṣad there underlies a hidden structural scheme. By deciphering the text with keen awareness and sensitivity one can avail himself of the key to the structural scheme and properly employing it, he can attune himself to the vision of the seer.

To unlock the mystery of existence pictured in *Aitareya Upaniṣad*, the commentator unravels the master key and uses it with contemplative skill which he himself inherited from his own master Nataraja Guru, who was a direct disciple of Narayana Guru himself.

In the present one the commentator does not conform himself fully to the traditional style of others in the same field. He also takes meticulous care not to tresspass the structural limits of thought depicted in it. The author rather employs his knowledge of psychology, philosophy, modern science and above all common sense to discuss the subtle ties in elaborate detail.

I hope this may be of much help to the earnest seekers of truth.

Sadhu Sudhakara Saukumarya

Contents

Introduction

INDIA'S civilisation is like a great banyan tree. It assimilates all the nourishment it needs for sustenance from the Upaniṣads, a source that has remained ever undiminished. The way life is viewed in the Upaniṣads has become absorbed into the fabric of the civilisation of India so universally that even illiterates are soaked in its essence, yet they remain oblivious of being so. Only when by chance one comes upon an Upaniṣad and he gets familiar with its way of thinking that he realises that his being is already inbued with its essence.

Reality and the actualities of life, as seen by the Upaniṣads, are not two. They portray the various facets of the actualities of life in terms of Reality, or Reality in terms of the actualities of life. In ordinary life what matters is our personal beingness and its pleasures and pains, as well as how we react to each other.

The life principle, known in Sanskrit as *prāṇa*, is supposedly the epicentre of life's activities. *Prāṇa*, literally meaning breathing, has the air we inhale and exhale for its basis. The function of *prāṇa* is impossible without the surrounding air. This air could thus very well be considered the epicentre of life. It is a vital part of our physical existence, not merely when breathed in but even as the air surrounding our body, which extends upto the boundless atmosphere, making the physical existence of each one of us likewise extensive in dimension. To distinguish between the individual aspect of the function of air and its universal counterpart thus becomes rather difficult. It would be easier to conceive the two as opposite poles of one existential situation, that of the air principle. As a living entity, its individuated aspect is marked by the respiratory function. As a cosmological phenomenon, life should have in it a cosmic respiratory function also, though this is beyond the grasp of the human mind. The atmosphere then should also have an alternating respiration-like function within itself.

Life is multi-faceted. Each facet of it, like that of the respiratory function, could too be seen as having similar opposite poles — one relating to the individual entities and the other to the universal where total being becomes the matter of concern. For example, eyes in individual beings have the sun for their universal counterpart. The former aspect in Sanskrit is known as *vyaṣṭi*, the latter, *samaṣṭi*. Looking at the overall scheme of life as having two opposite facets at its every phase, is the approach that dawned upon the *ṛṣi* of the *Aitareya Upaniṣad*.

Every Upaniṣad is appended to one or other of the four Vedas, the most ancient basic scriptures of India. The Upaniṣads, for this reason, used to be called Vedāntas meaning they constituted the concluding part (*anta*) of the Vedas. The philosophical implications of these words — *vedas*, *upaniṣad*, *vedānta* — having already been sufficiently clarified in our comments on the *Kena-Upaniṣad*, are better not repeated here.

The *Aitareya Upaniṣad* forms part of the *Aitareya-Āraṇyaka* as its Chapters IV, V, and VI, which is a continuation of the *Aitareya Brāhmaṇa*, all appended to the *Ṛgveda*. The *ṛṣi* who revealed them as the verbal expression of the intuitive vision he had, was Aitareya Mahīdāsa who lived in the Kuru-Pāñcāla region, and from him the Upaniṣad derived its name. A reference to him the *Chāndogya Upaniṣad* (III.xvi.7) says, he lived till he was 116. He, according to Madhva, was the son of Viśāla and was the incarnation of Viṣṇu. Sāyaṇa, the famous commentator on the Vedas, tells an interesting story about Mahīdāsa:

Mahīdāsa was born of a woman known as Itarā, meaning 'the other woman', and hence the name Aitareya, literally, born of Itarā. Mahīdāsa's mother, presumably not the legitimate wife of his father, was therefore denied the rights and privileges of a wife. Once, a great fire-sacrifice (*yajña*) was held in which Mahīdāsa's father was the *yajamāna* (the one who performs and pays for a sacrifice. The *yajamāna*'s son normally would be allotted his rightful seat in the hall (*yajñaśālā*), but Mahīdāsa was denied that seat. Taking it as an insult on her, Itarā prayed to the Goddess Earth (Bhūmī Devī, also called Mahi), her favourite goddess, for atonement. Gratified, the Goddess appeared, and seating Mahīdāsa on a celestial throne, taught him the supreme wisdom. Becoming thus a *jñānin* and one of the most honoured *ṛṣis* (seers), Aitareya revealed the scriptures now known as the *Aitareya Brāhmaṇa, Aitareya Āraṇyaka*, and *Aitareya Upaniṣad*. A disciple of Mahī, he became famous as Mahīdāsa, *dāsa* meaning servant.

The evils and senselessness of a caste-based social system are what this story points to. Itarā presumably was a śūdra woman and hence unacceptable to the brāhmaṇa wives of Viśāla; so she was relegated as 'the other woman'. Her son Mahīdāsa was denied his rightful seat in the *yajñaśālā* (the hall of fire-sacrifice). But Aitareya, by revealing the supreme wisdom through one of the most important Upaniṣads along with the connected Brāhmaṇa and Āraṇyaka, proved his worth and testified the meaninglessness of caste-based social concepts and prejudices.

What all the Upaniṣads try to do is to reveal through the medium of words the Supreme Wisdom that is really inneffable. Nevertheless, the *ṛṣi* of each Upaniṣad has his own way of visualising the Reality and thus his own way of presenting it. The *Kena Upaniṣad*, for example, reveals it as answering the question, "What impelling force works behind all the throbbings of life?" The problem of death and the state after it, is what becomes instrumental in the *Kaṭha Upaniṣad*. The present Upaniṣad, on the other hand, portrays in a rather poetically picturesque way how the mysterious phenomenon of world and life, with their universal and particular aspects of existence, get unfolded from the one primeval causal Reality (*ātman*), and finally how *ātman* perceives itself as the one underlying substance of all such phenomena.

॥ ॐ ॥

Peace Invocation

शान्ति पाठः

ॐ वाङ् मे मनसि प्रतिष्ठिता मनो मे वाचि प्रतिष्ठितमाविरावीर्म एधि। वेदस्य म आणीस्थः श्रुतं मे मा प्रहासीः अनेनाधीतेनाहोरात्रान् सन्दधामि। ऋतं वदिष्यामि। सत्यं वदिष्यामि। तन्मामवतु तद्वक्तारमवतु। अवतु मामवतु वक्तारम्॥

ॐ शान्तिः शान्तिः शान्तिः॥

aum̐ vāṅ me manasi pratiṣṭhitā, mano me vāci pratiṣṭhitam; āvir āvīr ma edhi: vedasya ma āṇīsthaḥ। śrutam̐ me mā prahāsīḥ। anenādhītenāhorātran samdadhāmi, ṛtam̐ vadiṣyāmi। satyam̐ vadiṣyāmi। tan mām avatu, tad vaktāram avatu, avatu mām, avatu vaktāram avatu vaktram। aum̐, śāntiḥ, śāntiḥ, śāntiḥ ॥

My speech is well-founded in mind.
My mind is well-founded in speech.
O the self-evident, become self-revealed to me.
(Both mind and speech) be the linch-pin of my knowledge.
May my learning not leave me.
(For) by my learning indeed
I manage my days and nights
I'll speak out truth.
I'll speak out the true.
May that protect me.
May that protect my mentor.

Please protect me. Please protect my mentor.
Om Peace! Peace! Peace!

An attempt to reveal the secret wisdom of the Upaniṣads is the venture we are entering into now. The ultimate goal of all the Upaniṣads is one and one alone: safeguarding seekers from all sorts of fear. No one is afraid of oneself. Fear is always of someone else. Fear vanishes on realising that nothing that we can treat as 'other' exists anywhere. Though appearing in many forms, that which exists is one Reality alone. Oneself and all else are thus one Reality alone in essence. As the Substance of one's own beingness, it is called *ātman* (the Self); as the Substance of the beingness of everything, it is *Brahman*. Knowing that this *Brahman* or *ātman* alone, *nothing else*, exists, in oneself, in everything, is *brahmajñāna* or *ātma-jñāna* — a realisation that turns out to be absolute fearlessness as well. *Brahman* for this reason is even defined as fearlessness (*abhayam*). A prayer for the attainment of this goal, of finding one's own beingness in what really exists in oneself, thus attaining fearlessness, is at the heart of this Peace Invocation.

Language is the usual medium for the communication of ideas, words, spoken or written, forming the body of most languages. Symbols of visual import may also at times take the place of words. Such symbols, occupying the core of ordinary languages, enhances the depth and broadness of communicability of words, even more so as poetical images; words, however, remain the main tool.

An indepth study of the way ideas, feelings, experiences, and the like, get processed, rendering them communicable, has been made by the Indian psychologists of olden days. They identified four different stages in the process: *parā*, *paśyantī*, *madhyamā*, and *vaikharī*. Any psychological function needs an underlying substance in which they can take place. It is named *parā* in the sense that it transcends everything conceivable and preceivable. Unconditioned consciousness in essence (*cid-vastu*), this *parā*, never remains inactive. Its activity finding expression as specific forms of life-pulsation, becomes *cetanā*, the individuated consciousness. The underlying Consciousness-Reality, always active, constantly produces within itself ever new manifestations, and thus feels the contentment of self-expression, of getting actualised all the potentials hidden in itself. This is the kind of vision the present

Upaniṣad is going to reveal. This stage of preceiving its self-actualisation is called *paśyantī*, literally that which perceives, so-called because all the ideas, images, and emotions and all like psychological states that arise and subside within oneself are directly perceived or rather felt, though often unwittingly, by oneself.

All such inner perceptions are personal experiences, uncommunicable as such. Yet an urge to communicate that which is felt within is also characteristic of the human mind. The ability to do this as well as the freedom one has with some familar medium to do so, varies from person to person. In order to be communicated to others, that which is perceived or felt within needs to get cast, again unwittingly, into some known mould or medium such as language, painting, sculpture, music or the like. There may be rare individuals who can concoct new media of their own. Whichever the medium, the process of casting an awareness or experience into the mould of a medium is inevitable. The caster is none other than the Consciousness-Substance. This casting process is known as *madhyamā*, literally the middle. Lastly, it results in the emergence of expressed forms of ideas and experiences, known as *vaikharī*. Though, usually translated as 'articulated word', in the present context it stands for all expressed forms of psychological states. The word has acquired the above popular meaning because language is the universal medium of communication.

All the Upaniṣads are verbal expressions of an intuitive vision of some ṛṣis. They thus are merely the *vaikharī* aspect, with the former three remaining hidden behind. Alternatively expressed, the words, the various ideas correlated, the interrelation between words and ideas, and many such peculiarities of expression together constitute the exposition of the ṛṣi's vision. These peculiarities get naturally so arranged in the text that, that very arrangement, when intuitively perceived, leads us back to the *madhyamā*, *paśyantī*, and finally to the *parā* aspect of the ṛṣi's vision. Our aim in this present study should be to attain to that vision with the words of this Upaniṣad as our instruments.

Practically, it is impossbile to confine the integrity and transparency of an experiential enlightenment within the bounds of verbal expression, for experiential awareness is boundless whereas words and their meanings have their own limitations. To the extent it goes beyond the limitation of words, a verbal expression could be considered as coming closer to the experiential vision.

Similarly, the connotation of a word need not necessarily be the same for different people. The dictionary meaning might be the same for all, but how it is assimilated into one's own being varies. A lotus, for example, might be felt by two in two different ways: In the case of one who once had got stuck in the muddy bottom of a lotus pond while trying to pluck flowers, the meaning aroused by hearing the word 'lotus' would have the colouration of that bitter experience. How different is the impression in the mind of one who has experienced the sweeter aspects — the fragrance, gentle subtle colour, beauty, and so on — unique to the lotus! Thus, the impression a word creates in each person will be different, though not differentiable. A reader or student, in order to be able to attain to the very same inner vision the *ṛṣi* had, needs to have the same kind of transparency and purity of mind as the *ṛṣi* had while uttering those words. But already conditioned is each mind with various acquired and inherited propensities, preconceived ideas, and prejudices, all colouring all newly acquired knowledge. Such impurities need to be washed out before the dawning of the transparent vision of *ṛṣis* can happen. This is the purification of mind, known as *citta-śuddhi*, that is to be accomplished by spiritual disciplines known as *sādhanas*. Only then would the seer's words help reveal in us the original vision he had had. Pertaining to this, we discover, are the first two lines of the present Peace Invocation: "My speech is well-founded in mind. My mind is well-founded in speech". Even with ordinary words, what enables them convey some idea is the inseparability of words and meanings, an inseparability compared by the famous Indian poet Kālidāsa to that of Śiva and Pārvatī. At the beginning of his epic poem *Kumārasambhava*, he in the form of a propitiatory prayer says:

> Similar to the inseparable oneness of words and their meanings in the context of word-import, is the oneness of Śiva and Pārvatī, the parents of the world. Salutations to them!

The prayer, "O the self-evident, become self-revealed to me" may sound like a conundrum. The original word *āviḥ* means, that which is perceptible just in front of oneself. Why should such an entity become revealed again?

What all the Upaniṣads ultimately aim at is the attainment of life's fulfilment through directly perceiving the one immortal Reality that underlies everything, as the meaning of one's own beingness. That Reality — *Brahman* — it is that assumes the form of ourselves as well as of the world around us. This certainty attained, one begins to see *Brahman* alone in all the ever changing appearances.

Yet our living is not at all guided by this awareness. Instead, we consider ourselves as observers, the subject, and the world around us as the observed object existing different from us. Such objects constitute also the field of our activities aimed at enjoying them. The events that take place in that objective world, when conforming to one's personal interests and convenience, are admitted as pleasurable, whereas the unfavourable and inconveninent ones are treated as painful. The intensity of that painfulness may at times go to the extent of cursing everyone else, oneself, or even God. The error we commit on such occasions is that of viewing life from the point of one's personal interests. Viewing thus from a point of very limited range of vision, we do not consider the interest of total life, and so become incapable of perceiving the one immortal Reality. A veil made up of our personal interests, so to speak, thus overcovers us leaving us oblivious of the one Reality that is open before us everywhere. It is only perceptible to those who are pining for it, only to those who are yearning to know the Reality behind all appearancess, and that too only when all the circumstantial factors are favourable. A true seeker, for example, need not necessarily find a true guide or *guru*, or compelling circumstances may leave his life's goal unfulfilled. The seeker in no way having any control over, such circumstantial factors have to become agreeable somehow, dictated as though by the will of nature or God. The yearning on the part of the seeker and the favourable circumstances provided by the chance element, come together and become one, thus result in unveiling the Reality already before him. Then only is it revealed that what appears as I — the knower, the doer of actions, and the enjoyer — and as the knowable and enjoyable world, are nothing but one Reality varioulsy manifesting. This awareness attained, one will no more be overjoyed by pleasurable events, nor grieve over painful events. Instead, an equanimity that faces all such events with a *yogī*'s mind becomes natural, seeing each event as a new facet the one Reality assumes while self-manifesting. The present prayer for getting the self-evident Reality self-revealed, implies all this.

This certitude gives us a firm ground in life. Searching for Reality is what all sciences do, each having their own field of enquiry whose bounds no science is willing to cross. The result is that an indepth knowledge of each science endows us with a different notion of life, none providing us with an over-all vision. Once an integral vision becomes available and attained, all the different fields of enquiry and the notions they provide achieve unity, each becoming a view of Reality from a particular angle, while adding to the holistic vision, each science thus gaining a new dimension, a new value.

A skilled joiner joins different wood pieces together positioning them appropriately and nailing them down, to serve one final purpose. Similarly, the philosophical vision unravelled here serves as a nail that holds together the otherwise divergent fields of knowledge. Hence the prayer: "Both mind and speech be the linch-pin of my knowledge". The science this Upaniṣad teaches — *brahmavidyā* — is the Science of sciences, that holds together all sciences, as belonging to one whole, each thus making life more meaningful. If such a Science of sciences is lacking, different sciences go different ways, one vying with another, and each sowing a different seed of peril. The freedom man has to choose, may be the greatest bane in human life, but also the greatest of all boons.

Education, for the modern man, provides the necessary background to secure a respectable job; the higher the respectability the less the quantum of physical work the job involves. Such education gained as a means to acquire particular jobs in most cases does not find any place of value in actual life. One who has graduated in Economics, for example, may get the job of a bus conductor or an office clerk, where nothing related to the science of Economics is of any use. The unbridgeable gap that thus develops between what one knows as one's potential and what one ends up doing, often results in eventual psychological maladjustments — one of the reasons why psycho-pathological cases are more frequent among the well educated than among others. What one learns in short should befit his personal character and should not drift away from actual life. The next prayer therefore is: "May not my learning leave me".

Śruta means that which is learnt. What is going to be learned in the present science — *brahmavidyā* — is no skilled knowledge on any particular subject. It, on the other hand, is the total awareness of the whole of life, the meaning of life. Nor is it meant for demonstrating in an examination, simply to be forgotten thereafter, or to be easily quoted when occasions arise to display one's own knowledgeability. It is simply an inner transparence that makes each moment we live meaningful and purposeful, where knowledge does not leave our living. Giving emphasis to the inseparability of this wisdom from life is stated next: "By my learning indeed I manage my days and nights".

By the bringing together of wisdom and living, life assumes an order of its own, an order perfectly in tune with the total Reality, of which individuals and their knowledge, all are mere momentary manifestations. The functional system of the total Reality is called *ṛtam*. The words uttered by those who make their existence fully in tune with *ṛtam* will also be likewise. Those words, imbued as they are with the spirit of the vision of one Reality (*satyam*) that underlies *ṛtam* become beacons for new seekers. For both the mentor and the student, the sole refuge is one Reality and the word that represents it. All this is implicit in the words: "I'll speak out Truth. I'll speak out the true. May that protect me. May that protect the mentor" Those who find refuge in *Brahman* become free of all the sufferings, whether self-caused, caused by other beings, or caused by providence.

PART I

Section One

ॐ आत्मा वा इदमेक एवाग्र आसीत्। नान्यत्किञ्चन मिषत्। स ईक्षत लोकान्नु सृजा इति।। १ ।।

aum ātmā vā idam eka cvāgra āsīt। nānyat kiñ cana miṣat। sa aikṣata lokān nu sṛjā iti ।। 1 ।।

Aum ātmā alone was verily the one that existed here in the beginning. Nothing rival whatsoever existed to blink. It thought: 'Let me now create the worlds'.

Idam (This)

Man, of all living beings, is considered the most advanced and the greatest because of his ability to acquire knowledge. The complexity of the structure of his brain has so developed that it inflames the urge for knowledge at the least provocation — the reason why biologists place man at the topmost rung in the evolutionary hierarchy. We need not treat this complex brain structure and the unique quality of the urge to know either as separately existing phenomena or as related as cause and effect. Rather, we will consider the two as two inseparable facets of the mysterious phenomenon called man.

Man, seeing anything, asks, 'What is it?', 'How is it?', 'Why is it?' The questions, 'What?', 'How?', and 'Why?' are thus the basic marks of human inquisitiveness. These questions are asked about everything man comes across. Yet he remains unsatisfied even on getting definite answers to all of them. An occasion, nevertheless, is there when he finds himself fully satisfied: when finding answers to these questions about himself!

Man, having no existence of his own apart from the cosmic system, is an inseparable part of it. Any attempt to know oneself as an entity existing on its own, therefore, results in no proper understanding of oneself. Man is part of the world; his life is part of the eternal flux. The proper knowledge one acquires about oneself should therefore be the knowledge of the everchanging world as well. The answer to the questions, 'What?', 'How?', and 'Why?' about oneself answers the same questions about the world also, for, in essence, the world and I are not two. Oneself and the world together, when considered as an object of enquiry, is signified by the word *idam* in the Upaniṣads, literally meaning 'this', but rendered here as 'here'. The present Upaniṣad is an attempt to answer the questions, 'What'?, 'How?', and 'Why?' of 'this'.

Undeniable is the existence of 'this', even as my own existence is. What really is the essence of this existence? Is it as we perceive it? Everything perceptible is evanescent; nothing remains permanent. Yet the world's perceptible existence continues unceasing like an eternal flow, comparable to that of a river. The eternal continuance of the flow needs a water-like substance making it possible. No water, no flow. When water is there, there appears the flow, along with the invincible current, whirlpools, waves, foam, and many such apparent aspects. What is the substance that underlies the mysterious eternal flow of the world with all its multifarious appearances? Knowing this one substance is the final goal of all scientists, all philosophers. If such a substance exists, it should have been the original cause of the world. Senseless is it to think of the non-existence of such a substance, for the simple reason that the flow exists. The Upaniṣads prefer to use the word *agre* (in the beginning) signifying this original cause.

Accustomed as we are to the time concept, the words 'in the beginning' may tempt us to think of a time when creation of the world happened. What time is, we are also not sure about. Our concept is that all events take place in time. Imagine a state in which no event occurs, where the world stands still. We will feel no passing of time then. Even our own feeling of being is a succession of events. Time is sensed only when events are there. It arises as events are sequentially ordered in our memory. Events in their turn take place only in an already existing world. Before the creation, if any, of the world, there was no time. It must then have been in a state of timelessness that creation took place, and the word *agre* (in the beginning) signifies it.

This notion is not quite unacceptable to modern science. Scientists' surmise is that the world began to exist with a great explosion called the Big-Bang. There was no time, no space, no matter before that. (That one should not ask, 'What was the thing that exploded?' is an accepted convention among theoretical physicists who work in the field.) Mysteriously enough, all the galaxies in the cosmos were found to be fast flying apart. This process must have had a beginning, and it should necessarily be a point — a point which contained in it the entirety of the enormous energy now spread out all over the cosmos. With that explosion arose matter, time, and space. The explosion thus did not take place at any point in time, because there was no time then. The scientists do not believe that this expanding process can go on endlessly either. There will be a time when the process is reversed, when the cosmos begins to contract, finally ending up at a point through a big implosion which they name the Big-Crunch — a point of re-emergence of matterlessness, spacelessness, and timelessness!

All such conjectures remain yet to be proved or disproved scientifically, as is the concept of the *ṛṣis* that *ātmā* alone existed in the beginning. Be that as it may, what is significant in this context is that the beginning conceived of is not a temporal one. It is something beyond, inconceivable though. Mythological legends of India refer to this beginning as *kalpādi* and the end of the world *kalpānta*.

What did exist at such a beginning as the causal substance? Or, what was the primeval cause of all phenomenal becoming? The Upaniṣads answer the question differently themselves. The *Chāndogya Upaniṣad*, for example, says, '*sat* (Existence alone was here, O dear, in the beginning' (*sad eva somya idam agra āsīt* — VI.ii.1). Seemingly contradicting it, the *Taittirīya Upaniṣad* proclaims: "This remained indeed *asat* (non-existent) in the beginning" (*asad vā idam agra āsīt* — II.vii.1), whereas the present text emphatically says, "*ātmā* (the Self) alone was, verily, the one that existed here in the beginning". Do these apparently different Upaniṣadic utterances signify the same inner vision? If so, why are they so mutually exclusive, at least in appearance? These questions had always been brain-teasing for commentators. Not interested in such polemics, we may focus rather on what that causal substance, acceptable alike to scientists, thinkers, and *ṛṣis*, is.

Despite such differences in introductory statements, that *ātmā* (the Self) is the one Reality that underlies all appearances, is the basic stand all the Upaniṣads agree on. The word *ātmā* too, as used in the Upaniṣads often varies in its nuances. At times, it is used to denote the life-principle in all individual living beings having the sense of being, the doer of actions, and the knower and enjoyer of objects. The word *ātmā* in this sense derives from the verb root *at*, meaning 'to eat', 'to enjoy'. *Ātmā* then is that which eats or enjoys (*atti iti ātmā*), a concept rather akin to the soul concept of Christian Theology. Even the physical body is referred to, though rarely, as *ātmā* in the Upaniṣads. The sense metaphysically that is most sound and fully in line with Vedānta's stand is, the Reality or Substance that pervades all appearances, even as gold-substance pervades the being of ornaments, or water the being of waves. The word *ātmā* in this sense derives from the root *āt*, meaning to pervade (*ād vyāpane*), which is a secondary root derivation from the original root *at*, meaning always reaching everywhere (*aṭa sātatya-gamane*). *Ātmā* in that sense is the one substance that unfolds itself as everything. It, as the indwelling Reality that controls the becoming of all appearances, is often referred to as *antaryāmin*. What this Reality is in essence is a bone of contention among scientists and thinkers alike. Whatever Its nature conceived by them, It necessarily has to be one that can assume the form of the subtlest animating principle as well as the grossest physical body of all beings. Albeit, the simplest meaning of the word *ātmā* is 'I'. The real search for the real content of 'I' or oneself solves all the problems.

The Original Cause, as Science Views It

The unproved notion that all phenomena in nature are caused by matter rules over the entire realm of modern science. Attempts to trace the original cause of the universe are made on that same basis. Is matter an objective gross entity, or is it merely conceptual? Scientists and philosophers of science are divided on this issue. To occupy space and to have mass are considered two defining qualities of matter. What is the substance qualified by these qualities? To answer this question, scientists go to the atomic and subatomic levels of existence of matter.

Those who consider matter as a gross entity think of it as the concretised form of energy, an entity which is not gross at all. Energy exists in the form of tiny particles, which scientists call the 'building blocks of the universe'. As particles they are concrete entities, though inconceivably small. As energy they are not so, but are wave-like. And both theories were scientifically proven. Finding no way to reconcile these two mutually exclusive conclusions, they had to admit an element of indeterminism or uncertainty in this realm, which eventually assumed the status of a scientific theory with the sonorous name 'the theory of indeterminism' or 'the principle of uncertainty'. Scientists, when applying this as a scientific theory, are ignoring the basic stand of science that no theory will be considered a theory unless it explains the concerned phenomenon reasonably. The scientists had to admit this uncertainty when they found that determining simultaneously the velocity and position of these constantly moving energy particles was impossible: when the velocity is determind the position becomes uncertain; when position becomes certain its velocity goes uncertain. With the detection of various types of such sub-atomic particles such as electron, proton, neutron, positron, mison, gluon, quarks, photon, pion, seeing them all as apparent manifestations of one energy became a necessity. Not only the subatomic energy, but the entire energy of the cosmos also had out of necessity to be seen as homogeneous. The scientists put energy into four categories: gravitational force, electro-magnetism, weak-nuclear force, and strong-nuclear force. A grand unification theory was conceived with the intention of bringing all four into its fold. But one — the gravitational force — was unwilling to step into the fortress of the grand theory. It is still remaining outside. Scientists have not given up the hope of finding a way to widen the theory so as to accommodate the rebellious one as well. This done, they think, the Unified Field Theory dreamed of by Einstein will become an accomplished fact. Scientists, novertheless, do not have any compunction in equating matter with energy with the famous Einsteinian formula $E = mc^2$ as its basis. This vast field of enquiry notwithstanding, 'What life is?' Still remains an enigma untouched by any such theories.

The Origin of Life

How did life originate? Would Life emerge if we could move back in time and let events unfold in the same setting, or if the setting were duplicated on some other planet? If so, would it be the kind of life we know or something different? These are questions science has so far admittedly failed to answer. What we have instead is a profusion of theories, slanted by scientific specialisations, philosophical attitudes, and ideological bias of their authors. Life-science, scientists admit, is in an embryonic stage, despite all the advances made by biology which virtually is the science of life. Any available scientific explanation of life's origin is in accord with the laws of physics and chemistry. Energy particles/waves form the substance of which all the worlds and life are constituted, as physics conceives it.

Each energy particle/wave belongs to a well-structured system called atom and is in a state of constant movement within that system. Any change in the pattern of the atoms' movement, any one being thrown out of the system, or any new one being allowed in, results in strong bonds among them, leading to the creation of molecules. The variety of such bonds could be countless; equally countless would be the variety of molecules thus created. Of such, one molecular structure known as DNA has in it the life principle as its peculiar quality, and a living organism is an aggregate of such molecules.

Study of subatomic particles, of atom and its structure, and of molecules and their structure, all form part of physics. Reaching the peculiar molecule called DNA we find ourselves, to our astonishment, as if by a quantum leap, landed in the world of biology where all the subatomic, atomic, and even molecular structures become irrelevant. DNA turns out here to be the smallest life unit, whose constituent parts are not atoms but genes, which in turn are information bits. What all such studies help us to have is merely a description of the minutest physical aspects of a living organism, never any explanation of what life is and how it originated.

Carbon, hydrogen, nitrogen, oxygen, phosphorus, and sulpher were detected to be sustaining elements; and as a result all search for the origin of life happened to be based on the notion that these were the life-originating elements. Under certain influences of electric charges, radiation, and other sources of energy, the atoms in their combinations were reshuffled to produce amino acids and other basic biological building blocks. Yet, how such building blocks turned out to play their central biological role is an intriguing question even to scientists.

Life or consciousness, as held by some scientists, is merely an epiphenomenon, a correlate of certain polyneural activities. Their explanation too varies from one scientist to another. Some do admit a life principle, though hesitantly, but with no explanation. How is it that so many scientists and cognitive scientists can say so many things about one thing: the origin of life? Nevertheless, the emergence of more and more 'isms' on this one problem, makes of scientific philosophy a graveyard of 'isms', and in no way makes the real origin more than one, which reality is still however not understood.

The views of scientists willing to cross the borders of the orthodoxy of monistic materialism are generally dismissed with an expression of amused tolerance by orthodox scientists and philosophers. Even those who admit that the universe looks more like a great thought than a great machine are there among those rebellious scientists. Those who do so do not find any scientifically tenable means to substantiate it. Nor are they willing to make a quantum leap to find themselves standing beyond the bounds of orthodox scientific thinking.

The *ṛṣis* of India, on the contrary, are already standing where those scientists are dreaming of reaching by a quantum leap which they are unwilling to take. The firmness of the *ṛṣis*' stance is in their finding themselves one with the mysterious reality they have arrived at. They look down with a sense of amusement at the world where scientists and philosophers are still struggling in their uncertainty, to reach where they already are. They see only one Reality as existing, as has always existed, and as will exist. It, in Its mysteriously creative self-unfoldment, appears as both mind and matter, as body and soul, as cause and effect, as subject and object. They call that Reality *ātmā* in the metaphysical sense already clarified. The *ṛṣi* of the present Upaniṣad therefore declares: *Ātmā* alone was verily the one that existed here in the beginning (*ātmā vā idam eka evāgra āsīt*).

Nothing Rival Existed

The problem as to whether the original causal substance, *ātmā*, is mind or matter in essence, does not arise at all in the present search, for the reason that what is searched for is the causal Reality behind *idam* (what is here) undifferentiated as mind and matter. Such preconceived notions as that matter is the cause of everything phenomenal as with modern science, did not vitiate the intuitive search of the *ṛṣis* for Reality. Any search with a prejudiced notion for its basis leads only to a prejudiced conclusion, never to an unprejudiced absolute certainty. Ever since man began to think he has been asking the question: "Does matter abide in mind or mind in matter?" As yet no tenable answer is available, and no one thinks of finding one in future. Vedānta, nevertheless, does not face the problem in its philosophy. That it has no right answer only because the question is wrong, would be a Vedāntin's natural reaction. The question is based on the misconception that what exists is divisible as matter and mind. No one asking the question cares to look back and ask themselves: Is it proper to divide reality as mind and matter? Only because of ignorance one divides the one reality into two and then asks which abides in which. This error unwittingly committed by everyone is known in Vedānta as *avidyā*. Its impact is so enormous that it misguides not only ordinary men but well-known philosophers and modern scientists also.

The one Reality, *cit* (consciousness) in essence, unceasingly creative — it cannot remain otherwise — has in it the urge for manifesting itself, resulting in the appearance of the world in Itself. What we call mind and matter are merely two extreme poles of the one context of self-unfoldment of *ātmā*; the invisible subtlest aspect of manifestation forming mind and the visible grossest forming matter. The two are not related as cause and effect. Wrongly we consider them as cause and effect simply because both appear simultaneously, but in different ways. The dissolution of the two also happens simultaneously. With this dissolution — what we call death — what really exists in what disappears does not cease to exist. *Ātmā* thus is the Reality that gives birth to both mind and matter and into which both get dissolved. It is a living Reality. The primary sign of life being blinking or pulsating, it says, 'Nothing whatsoever existed to blink' (*nānyat kiñcana miṣat*).

He Thought

The endlessly multifarious world of effects appeared in the one *ātmā* as a result of Its beholding or thinking. *Īkṣ* means to look at something intently, the intention here being nothing other than seeing Itself manifested as the world. A systematic unfoldment needs a thought behind it which knows, what is to be created, whence to create, how to create, and why to create. What is to be created is the world of mind and matter. *Ātmā* alone existing, nothing else was there out of which the world was to be created. Consciousness in essence, *ātmā* necessarily knows what can be created and how. This practicable resolve for self-unfoldment in a systematic way is known as *saṁkalpa* (practicable resolve) — an invincible resolve to actualise all the possibilities potent within, and thus to experience the contentment of self-expression. A child's playing with anything at hand, creating many things out of it, and immediately destroying them for the sheer joy of bringing out the creative potential within, could very well be compared to *ātmā*'s unfolding itself as the world and absorbing them back into itself. Narayana Guru confirms this stand when he says:

> To know itself and its own nature *ātmā* transforms itself as specific manifestations such as earth and other elements, which are like the tip of an everglowing fire-stick spiralling up, back and forth, and turning round.
>
> — *Ātmopadeśa Śatakam*, Verse, 33

Concerning *ātmā*'s thinking or beholding may arise a doubt: Where did *ātmā* behold? What did *ātmā* behold? *Ātmā* alone existing, there was nothing else to look at. *Ātmā*'s beholding should therefore be at itself. What one sees when looking at oneself will also be oneself. *Ātmā* alone existed, it looked at itself, and as a result emerged the world. *Ātmā*, finally when the Upaniṣad concludes, looks around at the world thus created and sees nothing but itself appearing as the world. Anticipatory of this final conclusion is the beginning usage *īkṣata*.

The stance that the observer and the observed are inseparably one may not be welcome to the mechanistically biased way of thinking of modern science. Its method presupposes the existence of the observed world separate from the observer, and its working like a huge machine, man the observer, a miniature separable machine, forming part of the huge one. Being conscious is the only act the brain-machine has to perform. How did that machine acquire the capability to observe and study not only external objects but its own internal attitudinal changes also? It is the result of an evolutionary process that has been going on for millions and millions of years. The ultimate goal of all theories, including the theory of evolution, is to ascertain what was the original cause of the world, including the life-phenomenon. The brain that makes this effort is nothing but part of the evolving world, though considered separable. It, in effect, means, as a result of the very long evolutionary process, was evolved a brain that is capable of searching for the reality that evolves. The observing brain is thus a machine contrived by the world machine itself through its evolutionary process in order to know its own secret. The world itself, thus, the scientists claim, gets evolved as the observer, and observes itself! What Vedāntins hold is that the Self, the all-observing, and all-evolving Consciousness, transforms itself as the world and observes itself. The basic difference between the two is only in their verbal expression. The reality that underlies both remains the same, where the observer-observed duality and the cause-effect duality are meaningless.

The Worlds (*lokān*)

Ātmā first thought of creating the world. The original word for 'let me create' is *sṛjai*, a conjugation of the verb root *sṛj*, meaning an already existing reality emitting some new apparent form of itself, not the creation of something new. The reality that exists is *ātmā* and what is emitted of it is the world (*loka*). *Loka* means that which is looked at, and consists of the perceiver and the perceived. The world experienced by a perceiver is in the form of a mental image or percept that supposedly corresponds to the objective world. No way of knowing the world other than as a percept existing, checking how far the percept corresponds to the actual objective world is an impossibility. Every such percept is represented by a word or name. The subjective aspect of world experience thus consists of countless percepts and countless corresponding names. Countless corresponding objects added, complete the picture of the world. This picture is drawn by Narayana Guru thus:

> Names in their thousands,
> Percepts in their thousands,
> And the corresponding objects in thousands,
> Together constitute the world.
> —*Advaita Dīpikā*, Verse, 1

The world that emanated from the Self as a result of its thinking, was such.

स इमांल्लोकानसृजत। अम्भो मरीचीर्मरमापोऽदोऽम्भः परेण दिवं, द्यौः प्रतिष्ठाऽन्तरिक्षं मरीचयः। पृथिवी मरो या अधस्तात्ता आपः।। २ ।।

sa imāṁl lokān asr̥jata, ambho marīcīr maram āpo'do' mbhaḥ pareṇa divam; dyauḥ pratiṣṭhā, antarikṣam marīcayaḥ, pr̥thivī maro yā adhastāt tā āpaḥ ।। 2 ।।

He emitted the world: sky, light-rays, death, and water. Sky is beyond heaven; the heaven is its support. The light-rays form the atmosphere and death the earth. What is underneath is waters.

In this stanza is described the archetypal form of the world emanated from *ātmā*. What thus emanated was not just 'one world' but many worlds (*lokān*). *Loka*, meaning, as we know, that which is perceptible, is derived from the verb root *lok*, meaning 'to visualise' (*loka darśana*). What the *ātmā* did in order to emanate such a perceptible world from itself is *īkṣaṇa*, which also means perceiving (*īkṣa-darśane*). Yet the two perceptions are basically different: *īkṣaṇa*, the perception that resulted in the emanation of worlds, is an inner search for all the hidden potentials within; and *lokana* is the act of observing what is thus externally emanated. The archetypal perceptible world thus emanated externally from *ātmā* is the result of the inner search and thinking of the very same *ātmā*.

Sky, Light-rays, Death, and Water

Four are the phenomenal aspects which first emerged from *ātmā*: sky, light-rays, death or the earth, and water, all belonging to a hierarchical order, the first reaching up the highest imaginable realm and the last flowing down to the lowest levels. Light-rays (*marīci*) fill the interspace between sky and earth, which latter is also the realm of death (*mara*). The word *mara* in the Vedic jargon signifies death and the earth alike. It is in the earth that life thrives through death — to be more precise, through birth and death. Water flows downwards even to the extent of being hidden underneath the earth's surface, yet sustaining life. This hierarchical order admittedly does not go with the concepts of any known system of philosophy; it simply depicts an ordinary man's vision of worlds where nothing is excluded.

Still this hierarchical order has implicit in it a value world of its own, full of suggestions. That *ambhas*, though meaning sky as well as water, is underscored as beyond heaven while the very heaven is its support. Reaching heaven is the highest goal of Vedism. Literally meaning 'worthy of being a goal to be achieved', *ambhas* stands for the ultimate goal of Vedānta — the realisation of the Absolute, the one Reality that underlies all the worlds including heaven. It thus is beyond heaven while being supported by heaven. Vedānta, though derived from Vedism, goes much beyond in its goal: the aim of Vedism is reaching heaven and that of Vedānta, reaching *Brahman*, symbolised by *ambhas* (sky) which therefore is poetically conceived as supported by heaven.

The two words *divam* and *dyau* are used here to mean heaven. Literally, both mean the abode of gods (*devas*). *Devas*, as relevant in the life of human beings, are the instruments such as sense-organs that help consciousness find self-expression in the form of some perceptual experience. (The word *deva* means 'that which is effulgence in essence.') All such experiences have their being in consciousness, the esential content of *ātmā*. Any actualisation of such experiences in consciousness needs the instrumentality of senses which include mind as well, and senses or *devas* in that sense always remain support to consciousness. This could also be construed as suggested in the concept of sky being supported by heaven.

The basic elements constituting the actual world are yet to emerge from the cosmic person (*puruṣa*) whose emenation also is to happen from waters, as will be stated in the stanzas coming up. Therefore, the four factors that have already emerged do not represent anything in the actual world; they are mere symbols of the primeval stage of the emenation of a living world from *ātmā*. Similar are they to the molecular soup conceived of by modern science as the genesis of life. The Rāmānuja School of Vedānta and Purāṇas (mythological legends of India) alike hold that *Brahman* is Nārāyaṇa or Viṣṇu himself. From his navel he created the four-headed god Brahmā, and entrusted him with the duty of creating the actual world. The formulation of such imageries may have had the backing of the vision contained in the beginning stanzas of the present Upaniṣad where also the first emanation as part of creation is four-headed.

Underneath heaven that supports the transcendental sky, is the world of light-rays (*marīci*), the world of pure light where luminaries shine. This region, it says, is nothing but atmosphere (*antarikṣa*). *Antarikṣa* is so named because *ṛkṣas* (luminaries) are moving round within (*antar*) it. Experienced by us as one though, *antarikṣa* has multiple luminaries shining and moving within it. It symbolises the one boundless consciousness within which manifest luminous, countless specific forms of knowledge. The sky (*ambhas*) thus stands for the unconditioned Consciousness and light-rays for the innumerable specific forms of knowledge that get formulated within It.

Below the atmosphere comes the earth. *Mara,* meaning death and earth alike, is equated to *pṛthvī*, again meaning the earth. The earth is the realm of horizontally spread out beings having birth and death, and *pṛthvi,* literally, is that which is spread out. It is the realm of beginningless and endless manifestations, even though the actual surface of the earth is not boundless geographically speaking. It is among living beings that the phenomenon of appearance and disappearance is quite apparent, and life is sustained by water. Vegetables, which all living beings depend on for food, sucks in water from the underground rather than from the surface, and the underground water is available everywhere, suggested by the plural usage 'waters'. Water thus symbolises the causal source of all life manifestations. The hierarchical order visualised here thus consists of the causal source beneath, the horizontally spread out manifestations above it, the realm of multiplicity of specific knowledges still above, and the unconditioned awareness of the non-dual Reality at the top.

A horizontal line across the centre of the vertical series drawn, the bottom region would be seen predominant in the existential (*sat*) aspect, and the top one in the knowledge (*cit*) aspect — the former formed of *ambhas* (sky or water) and *marīci* (light-rays) and the latter of *āpaḥ* (waters) and *mara* (death or the earth). Light-rays and the earth, the realms of multiplicity, one of knowledge and the other of beings, come together and coalesce in the middle from the two sides. The two extremes, on the other hand, are of all inclusive oneness. That the two are non-dual in essence is symbolised by the water factor common to both, *ambhas*, meaning also water in the sense that its flow reaches everywhere. *Ambhas*, representative of the ultimate goal and *ap* representative of causal substance, in essence are thus one water, the former in a subtle form and the latter in gross form. Water, the common content of both, is the symbol of life force as well as viability.

Ap and *ambhas* being the two extremities, suggests also the indistinctness of both, the causal substance and the ultimate goal. The realms of multiplicity, of knowledge as well as of beings, alone are distinct.

The vertical series of the primary phenomenal becoming visualised here is thus highly symbolic of the various levels of becoming, the differentiating characteristics of each, the ultimate goal of life, the distinct and indistinct aspects of life, and many such, all melted into a sublime poetical imagery. The sweeter it is felt to be, the more it is meditated upon. Yet it is not a portrayal of the acutal world emanated, which is yet to come up in Stanza 4.

स ईक्षतेमे नु लोका लोकपालान्नु सृजा इति।
सोऽद्भ्य एव पुरुषं समुद्धृत्यामूर्च्छयत्।। ३ ।।

sa īkṣata ime nu lokā, loka-pālān nu sṛjā iti;
so'dbhya eva puruṣaṁ samuddhṛtyāmūrchayat ।। 3 ।।

He pondered : 'Worlds are here indeed. Let me now create their guardians'. Right from the waters he drew forth *puruṣa* and shaped him.

Loka (the world), having emerged, needs someone to do the *lokana* (looking at), or else it will not be *loka*, meaning that which is looked at. More than a mere onlooker, he will be the protector as well. Looking at is the function of *cit* (consciousness); how the world is looked at and looked after is dictated by the *ānanda* (contentment) content, for any deliberate move made by consciousness is a move to actualise *ānanda* in some way. It is this urge for *ānanda* that guides the moves and guards the world. The emanation of such a value-minded world-guardian, as part of the creation of the world, that which is depicted here, is nowhere else than from *ātmā*, *sat-cit-ānanda* in essence.

The idea with which *ātmā* meditated was that of producing many guardians of the world, as is evident from the plural usage *loka-pālān*, but what emanated first from waters was *one puruṣa* alone. The plural usage anticipates the emerging of many individual *puruṣas*, that come up for discussion in the second chapter. *Puruṣa*, as the guardian of the world, is thus to be conceived as having two facets: one, the universal, who looks at and looks after the entire universe, as though treating the world as its body, and two the particular, who cares for one's own individual beingness as part of the whole. The one *puruṣa* referred to here is the former, and was drawn forth from waters, the vital source-substance. This *puruṣa* is somewhat like forerunner to the actual emantion of the world, as the etymology of the word suggests. Of the many derivations available, the one that fits in well with the context is from the verb root *pur*, meaning 'to go in advance' (*pura agra-gamane*). That he is known as *puruṣa* as his existence is felt everywhere in the world, is yet another derivation. This cosmic person, in the *Brāhmaṇa* part of the Vedic literature, is called *virāṭ-puruṣa* (the person whose splendour radiates everywhere). *Ātmā* is unmanifest. Itself desiring to become manifested, has first to assume the role of the willing mind for the manifestation, which cosmic mind is named *virāt-puruṣa* in the *Brāhmaṇa*s and mere *puruṣa* here in the Upaniṣad.

Waters are the source from which the cosmic *puruṣa* was drawn forth as a result of *ātmā*'s performing *tapas*. Water symbolises the original source as we have already seen in our comments on the last stanza. The causal substance for the origin of the world needs to be something so flexible and pliable that everything, from mind to matter, from the subtlest to the grossest, is able to emerge from it. Water signifies that flexibility and pliability. The *puruṣa* referred to here is the personification of the willful universal mind that first emerged from the causal substance. This cosmic *puruṣa* and the individual *puruṣa*s yet to emerge are not different realities. The one cosmic mind, impelled by the creative urge within itself, gets manifested as many minds, personified as many *puruṣa*s.

तमभ्यतपत्तस्याभितप्तस्य मुखं निरभिद्यत, यथाण्डं; मुखाद्वाग्वाचोऽग्निर्नासिके निरभिद्येतां, नासिकाभ्यां प्राणः। प्राणाद्वायुरक्षिणी निरभिद्येतामक्षिभ्यां चक्षुश्चक्षुष आदित्यः कर्णौ निरभिद्येतां, कर्णाभ्यां श्रोत्रं श्रोत्ताद्दिशः। त्वङ् निरभिद्यत त्वचो लोमानि लोमम्य ओषधिवनस्पतयो। हृदयं निरभिद्यत हृदयान्मनो मनसश्चन्द्रमा। नाभिर्निरभिद्यत नाभ्या अपानोऽपानान्मृत्युः। शिश्नं निरभिद्यत शिश्नाद्रेतो रेतस आपः।। ४ ।।

tam abhyatapat । tasyābhitaptasya mukhaṁ nirabhidyata yathāṇḍam: mukhād vāg, vāco'gnir nāsike nirabhidyetām, nāsikābhyām prāṇaḥ, prāṇād vāyuḥ; akṣiṇī nirabhidyetām, akṣibhyāṁ caksuḥ, cakṣuṣa ādityaḥ; karṇau nirabhidyetām, karṇābhyām śrotram, śrotrād diśaḥ; tvaṅ nirabhidyata, tvaco lomāni, lomabhya oṣadhi-vanaspatayo; hṛdayaṁ nirabhidyata, hṛdayān manaḥ, manasaś candramā; nābhir nirabhidyata, nābhyā apāno 'pānān mṛtyuḥ śiśnaṁ nirabhidyata, śiśṇad reto, retasa āpaḥ ॥ 4 ॥

Upon him he brooded. Thus brooded on, his mouth got hatched, as if an egg. From the mouth emerged speech and from speech, fire. Nostrils got hatched; from the nostrils emerged breath, and from breath, air. Eyes got hatched; from the eyes emerged sight, and from sight, the sun. Ears got hatched; from the ears emerged hearing, and from hearing, cardinal directions. Skin got hatched; from the skin emerged hairs, and from the hairs, plants and trees. Heart got hatched; from the heart emerged mind, and from mind, the moon. Navel got hatched; from the navel emerged out-breath, and from the out-breath, death. The sex organ got hatched; from the sex organ emerged semen, and from the semen, water.

How the cosmic person (*virāṭ-puruṣa*) emerged from waters, symbolic of the virility of the source, was shown in the last stanza. The emergence of the world — the aggregate of countless entities of countless variety, including the guardians of all those entities — is to happen next from the *virāṭ-puruṣa*. The peculiarity of this step by step coming forth of the world is that, the original Reality — *ātmā* — which alone existed in the beginning, continues to exist assuming the newly emerging various forms, yet undergoing no intrinsic change, similar to gold existing with no intrinsic change despite all the forms it assumes as ornaments.

One basic question remains unanswered ever since man began to think: How do eyes have the capability to perceive something external?

So too, how do ears hear the external sound? The same question could be asked about all other sense faculties also. Part of the living being, sense faculties are subtle in essence, whereas the objects they come into contact with are external and part of the gross world. How do these two, extremely opposite in nature, get united causing the experience of sense perception? Nothing in common that makes them come together and merge, is perceptible in the two!

Indian thinkers did not find it a conundrum at all, for they did not think of sense faculties and sense objects as opposite in nature. The two, they hold, are simply subtle and gross manifestations of one and the same underlying substance. The physical world is constituted of five basic elements: space, air, fire, water, and earth. Each in its subtlest form becomes a sense faculty and in its grossest form the corresponding sense object. Earth, the grossest element of the world, for example, has smell for its differentiating quality. The sense organ nose that grasps smell is the manifestation of the very same earth in its subtlest form. The smelling faculty and earth, essentially one in content, contact each other and realise their real oneness, which realisation we consider as sense perception. So are the other sense perceptions. Sense contact, thus, is not the event of two entities, opposite in nature, getting united, but is the natural process of two apparent forms of one substance finding their real oneness. Space, and ears that hear sound, the differentiating quality of space, are also similarly related. So also are air and skin that feels air's touch, fire and the eyes that see fire's form, water and the tongue that tastes water. Space, air, fire, water, and earth together form the gross universal existence; the sense faculties of hearing, touching, seeing, tasting, and smelling form the subtle factors of individual living beings. The universal and the particular, the gross and the subtle, are thus inseparable apparent forms of one basic substance. Against the backdrop of this grand vision of the universal-particular unity, but with a wider scope, is to be seen the creation picture portrayed here in the *Aitareya Upaniṣad*. Related to the five sense perceptions are not the dual factors the *upaniṣad* takes into account.

A long line of functions beginning with speech and ending with procreation, — each having its own universal and particular aspects — is here depicted, all emerging from the one cosmic person (*virāṭ puruṣa*). The *virāṭ-puruṣa*, thus, stands for the cosmos in its undifferentiated state. All faculties were in him in a potential state. They, in their universal dimension, emerged first. The live source out of which a live cosmos is to emerge, the cosmic person, in his being has various limbs, each the source of a different cosmic phenomenon. Mouth, for example, we know, is the seat of speech; so is it with the cosmic person. The faculty of speech in an individual being is considered the subtle function of the cosmic phenomenon fire. The *ṛṣi*, with this scheme of things in mind, visualises: from the mouth of the cosmic person emerged the cosmic speech phenomenon; from it emerged fire, the universal physical seat of speech. This fire, transforming itself as speech again, will find its seat in the mouth of individual human beings, as we will see in the next stanza. Cosmic person's mouth → cosmic speech phenomenon → cosmological physical seat of speech (fire) → actual speech → mouth of the individual human being — such is the scheme of macrocosmic and microcosmic factors integrally conceived by the *ṛṣi* of the present Upaniṣad. This vision encompasses such spheres as speech, breathing, seeing, hearing, growth of hair, mind, death, procreation, though such spheres actually are innumerable. Fire, the sun, air, points of direction, vegetation, the moon, death, and water are the corresponding cosmological phenomena that emerged from the cosmic *puruṣa*.

How they found a common home in human figure, resulting in the creation of man, is detailed in the next section. Man thus is the individuated version of the cosmic *puruṣa*.

Section Two

ता एता देवताः सृष्टा अस्मिन्महत्यर्णवे प्रापतंस्तमशनापिपासाभ्यामन्ववार्जत्।
ता एनमब्रुवन्नायतनं नः प्रजानीहि, यस्मिन् प्रतिष्ठिता अन्नमदामेति।। १ ।।

tā etā devatāḥ sṛṣṭā asmin mahaty arṇave prāpatamstam aśanāyā-pipāsābhyām anvavārjat; tā enam abruvann, āyatanam naḥ prajānīhi yasmin pratiṣṭhitā annam adām eti ।। 1 ।।

The divinities (the cosmic phenomena) thus created fell headlong into the great ocean of chaos. He (the Creator) made him (the cosmic *puruṣa*) hungry and thirsty. To Him they (the cosmic phenomena) said: Find out for us a home wherein we may settle down and eat food.

The emergence of the cosmic phenomena, fire, the sun, air, the points of direction, vegetation, the moon, death, and water, representative of the entire range of natural phenomena, is what was portrayed in the last stanza. They, in the present one, are conceived of as divinities (*devatāḥ*) following the Vedic tradition, of which Vedānta is a revaluation. The Vedas conceive each of the natural phenomena as having a presiding deity, whereas in the Vedāntic context depicted here, the phenomena and divinities are thought of as one, forming the cosmological aspects of functional faculties in human beings. *Agni* (fire), for example, is the universal counterpart of the speech faculty in man. *Agni*, in other words, finds expression as fire in the cosmic system and as speech in man. Similarly, *āditya* appears in the cosmos as the sun and in man as his sight; *vāyu* as air in the universe and as the touch-sense in man; *dik* gets unfolded as points of the compass in the world and as the hearing faculty in man; *oṣadhi* finds expression in the cosmic order as vegetation and in man as hair; *candra* as the moon in the cosmos and as mind in man; *mṛtyu* as death in the world and *apāna* in man; *ap* as water in the world and as semen in man. The *virāṭ-puruṣa* being the cosmic counterpart of man, the individual, all the cosmological divinities are first thought of as emerging from him. *Devatā* literally means, that which is lustrous and hence worthy of worship.

Ātmā the original source, *virāṭ-puruṣa* (the cosmic person) that emerged from *ātmā*, his various limbs, though thought of as different, all are still mere principles existing in the realm of the intelligibles. Gross elements conceived here as emerging from the body of the *purusa* by the hatching of his limbs like eggs, are, on the other hand, visibly apparent.

Such gross elements, though apparent, do not form a world unless systematised into a cosmic order. Until this occurs, it would be as though they fell headlong into an ocean of chaos. This ocean (*arṇava*) need not necessarily be taken as that of *saṁsāra*, individuals' repeated turning round in worldly life, for, the individuals who are to undergo such a *saṁsāra* are yet to be created. The next step in the process of creation therefore is that of systematising the cosmic entities remaining in a chaotic state. Such a system must needs have well structured individuated entities constituting it, represented by the human figure here. Man's form thus represents individuated beings and a systematised cosmos alike. Entities chaotic in nature, when systematised, become cosmos. Man, the seeker as well as the individuated being, finds himself representing the cosmos. His coming into being thus stands for the creation of the world.

The chaotically existing elements to get systemised as the cosmos, need an inner urge for it; this is provided by *ātmā* itself in the form of hunger and thirst in the *virāṭ-puruṣa* which then rendered man's faculties and the corresponding cosmic elements restless. The hunger and thirst thus produced in the *puruṣa* are not merely the ones for food and drink with which we are familiar. They are instead to be understood in a broader sense. Fire's inner urge for getting transformed into speech in individual human beings, the sun's urge to become eyes and their sight in living beings, the inner urge in the directions of space for becoming transformed into the faculty of hearing and its sense-organ in individual living beings, the moon's urge to become mind capable of imagining and thinking in man, death's urge to become *apāna* the tool of dissolution of living beings, water's urge to become semen in male beings and thus ensure reproduction, and all similar urges for correlation between macrocosmic and microcosmic factors are symbolically represented by the present hunger and thirst.

Fire that emerged from the cosmic person is an abstract entity. Its becoming actualised in the world of life needs its concretisation in an individual being in the form of mouth and its faculty of speech. Air, the content of *prāṇa*, likewise, as the element emerging from the *puruṣa*, is an abstract entity that needs to manifest in individual beings in the form of their nostrils and their breathing power, in order to pulsate as life. All the cosmic elements similarly need concretisation and individualisation so as to have a stable functional basis, and that too a common one, seated on which they could satisfy their respective hungers and thirsts. All the divinities together therefore pray *ātmā*:

'Find out for us a home wherein we may settle down and eat food'.

ताभ्यो गामानयत्ता अब्रुवन्न वै नोऽयमलमिति। ताभ्योऽश्वमानयत्ता अब्रुवन्न वै नोऽयमलमिति।। २ ।।

ताभ्यः पुरुषमानयत्ता अब्रुवन् सुकृतं बतेति। पुरुषो वाव सुकृतम्। ता अब्रवीद्यथायतनं प्रविशतेति।। ३ ।।

tābhyo gām ānayat tā abruvan, na vai no'yam alam iti ।
tābhyo'śvam ānayat tā abruvan, na vai no'yam alam iti ।। 2 ।।

tābhyaḥ puruṣam ānayat tā abruvan, sukṛtam bateti, puruṣo vā va sukṛtam, tā abravīd, yathāyatanam praviśateti ।। 3 ।।

He led up the form of a cow to them. They said: 'This verily is not sufficient for us'. He then led up the form of a horse to them. They said: 'This too verily is not sufficient for us'.

He then led up a human figure to them. They said

joyously: 'Well done!' Human beings verily are well done (well created). He (*ātmā*) told them: 'Do enter your respective abodes in it'.

The divinities, so far roving with no abode to sit quiet and eat, are now given a common home — the human figure. First, they were offered a cow's form; they found it insufficient; then a horse's form which they also found inadequate. It was with the offering of the human figure that they felt satisfied. In exultation they exlaimed, "Well done!" Why were they so exalted? What they were offered was the best of all creations. They were allowed to enter it and find their respective abodes. This indicates the superiority of mankind among living beings, yet not merely the biologically conceived superiority as the being in which evolution has reached its maximum complexity.Vedānta, treating beings, living or non-living, as various manifestations of the one and only *ātmā*, does not consider one species superior or inferior to another. Man's real superiority is of another order and is implicit in the word *puruṣa* used here as denoting human beings.

The guardian of the world first created was also called *puruṣa*. The original intention of *ātmā* was not just to create one guardian of the worlds, but to create many guardians (*lokapālan*). The cosmic *puruṣa* was simply the first one thus created, the humans being the rest. Man thus is not just one of the creations; he is also the guardian of all creations, equal thus to the cosmic *puruṣa*. Man, the individual *puruṣa*, so to speak, is a replica of the cosmic *puruṣa*, a concept very similar to the biblical concept of God creating man in His own image.

Any guarding reguires a knowledge about what is to be guarded and how. The cosmic *puruṣa* as well as the individual *puruṣa*s must be blessed with that knowledge — a sort of justification for Madhva's stand that God and souls are related as original and reflections.

That the cosmic *puruṣa* the first creation and man the last creation are to be meditated upon as one *ātmā* in essence will be underscored in Section 3 later. It is the one and same creativity of one *ātmā* that finds expression as the cosmic and the individual *puruṣa*s. That man has in him this creativity at its maximum is what makes him superior to all other beings. Man's superiority, in other worlds, is in his ability to create a world of fantasies of his own, even as God creates the actual world. The endless world of man's artistic creation is its outcome. The excellence of man's artistic creation, therefore, depends on the extent to which it is a replica of the ineffable creativity of God. All these can be seen suggested when conceiving the heart of the cosmic *puruṣa* getting hatched to become the cosmic mind, from which is to emerge the moon, and finally the moon as entering the individual *puruṣa* to become his heart, as we will see in the next stanza, his mind becoming one with heart, thus capable of creating anything. Man is the one being in which all cosmic creativity and all the cosmic phenomena converge to assume a minuscular form.

अग्निर्वाग्भूत्वा मुखं प्राविशद्वायुः प्राणो भूत्वा नासिके प्राविशदादित्यश्चक्षुर्भूत्वा अक्षिणी प्राविशद्दिशः श्रोत्रं भूत्वा कर्णौ प्राविशन्नोषधिवनस्पतयो लोमानि भूत्वा त्वचं प्राविशंश्चन्द्रमा मनो भूत्वा हृदयं प्राविशन्मृत्युरपानो भूत्वा नाभिं प्राविशदापो रेतो भूत्वा शिश्नं प्राविशन् ।। ४ ।।

agnir vāg bhūtvā mukham prāviśad, vāyuḥ prāṇo bhūtvā nāsike prāviśad, ādityaś cakṣur bhūtvākṣiṇī prāviśad, diśaḥ śrotraṁ bhūtvā karṇau prāviśann, oṣadhi-vanaspatayo lomāni bhūtvā tvacam prāviśaṁś candramā mano bhūtvā hṛdayam prāviśan, mṛtyur apāno bhūtvā nābhim prāviśad, āpo reto bhūtvā śiśnam prāviśan ।। 4 ।।

Fire became speech and entered the mouth.
Air became *prāṇa* and entered the nostrils.
The sun became sight and entered the eyes.
The points of direction became hearing and entered the ears.
Plants and trees became hairs and entered the skin.
The moon became mind and entered the heart.
Death became *apāna* and entered the navel.
Water became semen and entered the sex organ.

तमशनयापिपासे अब्रूतामावाभ्यामभिप्रजानीहीति। ते अब्रवीदेतास्वेव वां देवतास्वाभजाम्येतासु भागिन्यौ करोमीति। तस्माद्यस्यै कस्यै च देवतायै हविर्गृह्यते भागिन्यावेवास्यामशनयापिपासे भवतः।। ५ ।।

tam aśanāyā-pipāse abrūtām āvābhyām abhiprajānīhīti. te abravīt, etāsu eva vām devatāsvābhajāmi, etāsu bhāginyau karomīti: tasmād yasyai kasyai ca devatāyai havir gṛhyate bhāginyāvevāsyām aśanāyā-pipāse bhavataḥ ॥ 5 ॥

Hunger and thirst said to Him (*ātmā*):
For us also, please find an abode.
He said to them: I assign you two a place within all these divinities, and I make you sharers with them.
Whatever divinity an offering is made to, therefore, hunger and thirst become partakers in it.

The divinities, asked thus to find their respective abodes in the human figure, now enter it, making of it a living human being. The process of their entering follows, in the reverse order, the same sequence in which they emerged from the cosmic *puruṣa*. The mouth of the cosmic *puruṣa,* for example, hatched and out of it emerged his speech. From his speech emerged fire, which in turn became the individual speech and entered his mouth. This shows how a human being along with his functional faculties, the cosmological elements, and the Creator of all these are integrally correlated giving perfection to the overall system of life. The way they are related is neither as the part and the whole nor as the qualified and the qualities. That the one Reality homogeneously underlies all the three is what correlates them. In other words, one Reality, in its self-urged creative unfoldment, microcosmically assumes the form of a human being, macrocosmically of the world, and causally of the Creator. The one common homogeneous substance in all three is none other than *ātmā* itself. Such dualities as the universal and the particular, the generic and the specific, the macrocosmic and the microcosmic, the gross and the subtle, subject and object, the internal and the external, cause and effect, are all thus perceived as finding their place inseparable from a structurally coherent life system. This corelatedness, put into a tabulated form, appears like this:

Cosmic puruṣa's limb	*Cosmic puruṣa's faculty*	*Cosmic element that emerges*	*Individual puruṣa's* faculty	*Individual puruṣa's* limb
Mouth	Speech	Fire	Speech	Mouth
Nostrils	*Prāṇa*	Air	*Prāṇa*	Nostrils
Eyes	Sight	The sun	Sight	Eyes
Ears	Hearing	Directions of space	Hearing	Ears
Skin	Hairs	Vegetation	Hairs	Skin
Heart	Mind	The moon	Mind	Heart
Navel	*Apāna*	Death	*Apāna*	Navel
Sex organ	Semen	Water	Semen	Sex organ

The world, so well structured, is not inert. It lives. To live means to undergo constant transformation, to be in a state of eternal flux. It is the creative urge within what exists that brings about this flux. This urge lacking, life becomes meaningless. It, in its most apparent form, in its crudest form, is visible in living beings as their hunger and thirst, the two basic feelings that impel man to hunt out new pastures of life activity. That such hunger and thirst formed part of the cosmic system was perceived in Stanza 1 of this Section, yet no seat was assigned to them, on creating individual beings. They, in Stanza 5, are complaining about it to *ātmā*. What *ātmā* in response does is not to assign any specific seat to them; instead they are asked to be seated in the entire body system and to be sharers in all other faculties. Hunger and thirst thus have no specific seat of their won; they are felt all over the body. Though satisfied by food and drink that first reach the stomach, their satisfaction is felt all through the body; their nourishment also reaches everywhere. The faculties in us such as sight, hearing, touch, *prāṇa*, and so on, were conceived each as a divinity (*devatā*). Their existence and proper function are made possible by the nourishment that reaches them through food and drink. The inner urge for seeing, hearing, and so on could well be conceived of as the flaming of a sacrificial fire. Each such fire or divinity that burns in every individual is to be satisfied by offering the corresponding fuel, the object, that forms part of the cosmos. All such processes need the sustaining nourishment that food and drinks provide with: the sense in which hunger and thirst become partakers in any offering made to any divinity. Vedic ritual also acknowledges this principle by always making public feeding a part of any fire sacrifice. Fire-sacrifice (*yajña*) performed with no feeding is denounced as *tāmasa* (dark and inert) by the *Bhagavad Gītā*, saying,

> That fire-sacrifice that is performed
> Not holding to Vedic injunctions,
> Not preparing food, not chanting *mantra*s,
> Not giving free gifts (*dakṣiṇā*),
> And with no faith,
> Is known as *tāmasa* in nature.
>
> — XVII.13

Section Three

स ईक्षतेमे नु लोकाश्च लोकपालाश्चान्नमेभ्य: सृजा इति।। १ ।।

sa ikṣateme nu lokāśca loka-pālāś cānnam ebhyaḥ sr̥jā iti ।। 1 ।।

He thought: Here are the worlds and their guardians. Let me now create food for them.

सोऽपोऽभ्यतपत्; ताभ्योऽभितप्ताभ्यो मूर्तिरजायत। या वै सा मूर्तिरजायतान्नं वै तत्।। २ ।।

so'po'bhyatapat: tābhyo'bhitaptābhyo mūrtir ajāyata, yā vai sā mūrtir ajāyatānnaṁ vai tat ।। 2 ।।

He brooded over waters. From waters so brooded over emerged a solid form. Whatever solid form emerged from (waters) indeed is food.

This third section of the first chapter, in its ten stanzas, shows how the enjoyables are created and how they are related to the enjoyers.

Here, in two stanzas, we are focusing on the creation of food (*annam*). This food is not merely the one we eat. Hunger and thirst having been allowed to have all the divinities or faculties together for their abode, the food created signifies that which is enjoyed by all the faculties. Each of the various senses and faculties is hungry in its own way, each in need of food. Mere presence of senses does not yoke them to their objects; this happens only when they are hungry, and then only the respective object becomes its food.

How, by the simple act of looking at or thinking of (*īkṣaṇa*), *ātmā* creates all the worlds from itself, was clarified in the third stanza of the first section. The same *īkṣaṇa* results here in the creation of food as well. Created, though, by such a simple act, it has a sequential order of its own, each stage emerging as a result of the very same *īkṣaṇa*. Conditioned as our minds are with the linear way of thinking, this sequence also might be misconstrued as a temporal, linear one. Time-sense arising out of events only, the original event that resulted in the creation of the world could not have taken place in time: a concept also acceptable to modern science. The sequential order of creation depicted here, as well as in other Upaniṣads, has, therefore, to be perceived as a non-temporal one. Instead of as a linear progression, it could more intuitively be perceived as a concentric, circular expansion, *ātmā* always remaining at the centre. The one *ātmā*, by the simple act of *īkṣaṇa*, first got expanded as sky, light-rays, death, and waters. From the waters emerged the cosmic *puruṣa* and from the cosmic *puruṣa*, the entire world of universal elements and the individual *puruṣa*s. The universal elements found their seat in the sense-organs and faculties of the individual *puruṣa*. These sense organs and faculties grew hungry. By each of these stages the creation picture gets expanded, and now we are near the periphery where food for the senses is going to be created, again by the very same act of *īkṣaṇa*. Senses try to sieze the food so created but they fail, for the food was as though running away from the senses on to the outer periphery, as we shall see in the next stanza. Creation thus reaches the extreme outer periphery by the emergence of food.

Seen as a causally related event, food's creation is explicitly stated here as caused by water. All foodstuff has to emerge either from water or with the help of water, as though they in essence are water solidified, and hence the depiction: "Food emerged from the waters brooded over by *ātmā*".

Water's role in this creation picture is a crucial one. The creation of the cosmic *puruṣa* was from waters, which process continuing, the emergence of the cosmic *puruṣa*'s sense faculties, cosmic elements, individual *puruṣa*'s sense faculties, and finally the individual and his hunger emerge. Now it says, the food that satisfies that hunger also emerged from the very same waters. Indirectly it says: Man and all the stuff he needs for his satisfaction have one primeval source of origin, represented here by waters. These waters are not the physical water we are familiar with; it is rather a symbolic water standing for the one self-generative homogeneous substance that underlies both the enjoyer and the enjoyed, the subject and the object, conceived, by the poetically rich mind of the *ṛṣi*. Water, of all gross elements, is the one with plasticity at its maximum. It can be shaped into any form, and therefore is good enough to be a symbol for the one Reality that creatively unfolds itself as everything. That water is the original causal substance of all creation is an idea as old as the pre-Socratic thinkers, in the West, Thales the most ancient of them. In India, a mythological symbol portrays Viṣṇu, just before the creation of the world, as having a yogic repose on a banyan leaf that floats over the waters of the great deluge. It may perhaps be a mythological representation of the rich philosophical vision epitomised here in the Upaniṣad.

The relationship between the enjoyer and the enjoyed, the subject and the object, is a dialectical one, symbolised here by hunger. Such relationship is possible only between things or entities of one homogeneous content. Welding together of two pieces of metal, for example, is possible only if they are of the same metal. Hunger, similarly, gets satisfied only by consuming, the organism's getting united with, the concerned food and nothing else. The unifying relationship likewise between senses and external objects — an action that constantly takes place in our sense perception of every kind — itself therfore is the proof of the existence of one homogeneous content underlying both, symbolically represented by waters here. *Puruṣa* emerged from waters; he becomes interested in objects emerged likewise from waters. Water makes their coming together and getting united in the actualisation of sense perception and enjoyment, possible and understandable.

तदेतदभिसृष्टं पराङत्यजिघांसत्। तद्वाचाजिघृक्षत्, तन्नाशक्नोद्वाचा ग्रहीतुम्।
स यद्धैनद्वाचाग्रहैष्यदभिव्याहृत्य हैवान्नमत्रप्स्यत्।। ३ ।।

tad etad abhisṛṣṭam parāṅatyajighāṁsat । tad vācājighṛkṣat tan nāśaknod vācā grahītum; sa yad hainad vācāgrahaiṣyad abhivyāhṛtya haivānnam atrapsyat ।। 3 ।।

> The food so created wished to flee away. The *puruṣa* sought to sieze it by means of his speech, but found himself unable to do so. Had he taken hold of it by speech, he would have had satisfaction just by uttering the word 'food'.

This and the ensuing seven stanzas together describe how the *puruṣa* who emerged from waters, tries to grasp and eat the fleeing food, a solidified form of the same waters. All efforts made by means of the faculties such as speech, *prāṇa*, eyes, ears, skin, mind, sex organs, failed. It was by means of *apāna* that it was finally taken hold of. *Apāna* is the vital air that moves downwards in a living being effecting the digestion of food. Food getting digested means its destruction or death, and hence death is conceived of as the cosmological counterpart of the *apāna*'s function in individuals' bodies. Attempted to be grasped by the *puruṣa*, food (therefore) flees away impelled by the instinct for self-preservations. A mouse's state when chased by a cat is comparable to it.

The *puruṣa*'s effort to grasp at for food is in order to ensure his continued existence as an individual; the food's fleeing away from *puruṣa* is also impelled by the very same impulse in it. All such entities strive always for self-preservation, even at the cost of the destruction of another, though their origin is from one source-Reality. This common content in all, the common source of all, is no material entity; for it is in essence *sat*, *cit*, and *ānanda*. *Sat* means undeniable and indestructible existence, *cit* means consciousness, and *ānanda* value experience. *Ānanda* is something to be experienced, something to be actualised. Every acstualisation has to be an existential one. All individual beings always strive towards actualising their own *ānanda* content in the realm of existence (*sat*), in order to render it into a real experience. All efforts towards this achievement are made consciously where the function of consciousness (*cit*) is unavoidable. All efforts in life, in short, are a coalescent actualisation of *sat-cit-ānanda*.

Such actualisation of one's own *ānanda* content can take either of the two courses: one, by perceiving inwardly the one common source, *ātmā*, at the centre of the circle, and identifying oneself with that Reality; the other, by looking externally at the periphery for food for sense-gratification. The former, achieved through one's meditative inlook, will be of eternal value, whereas the latter achieved with the instrumentality of sense organs and body, will be of fleeting value. The former is realised by real-seekers, the latter is attained by pleasure-seekers.

The individual *puruṣa*'s place in the grand circle of creation is very near to its periphery, away from the centre. For this reason, an ordinary man's leaning towards actualising *ānanda* in life would naturally be by acquiring objects — represented by food — available nearby. Food, by giving satisfaction to living beings, necessarily dies out. No living being likes to be destroyed, food no exception. Getting away, food therefore tries to rescue itself from death. That appeasing hunger involves destruction of food is a law of life. Every search for sense gratification being an attempt to appease some hunger, all such actualisation of *ānanda* involves a sort of death of the object concerned. Death and actualising *ānanda* through worldly means, in this particular sense at least, are dialectical counterparts; perhaps one of the visions behind the Indian concept of Bhadrakālī, the Goddess in her terrible black form. Yet the word *bhadrakālī*, literally means, the auspicious black one, *bhadra* meaning the auspicious, and *kālī*, the black goddess. The allusion to death at the periphery of the grand creation circle could also be taken as suggestive of the outer limit of the expanding creation process. Death, always involved in sense gratification, at times may also rouse man to turn his search for *ānanda*, towards the centre of the circle, towards the immortal *ātmā*.

The individual *puruṣa* attempted to get at the fleeing food with his speech, but did not succeed. Had he succeeded, he would have been able to appease his hunger just by uttering the word 'food'. He tried to get at food also with *prāṇa*, eyes, ears, and all the other faculties, but in vain, except on trying with *apāna*. Śaṅkara thinks, the *puruṣa* did not know how to seize food. The cosmos created by the cosmic *puruṣa* from himself, as we know, has a structural perfection of its own, fully known to him. The individual *puruṣa* being a replica of the cosmic *puruṣa*, considering him to be ignorant of how his own faculties function is not sustainable. Be it as it may, we are sure of one thing: we can see food, smell food, touch food, hear food, and know food in many ways; yet the real appeasing of hunger happens only on eating it. Eating means making it part of our being by digesting, a process facilitated by the downward moving vital air (*apāna*). So natural is this nutritive system that we do not even ask, why it is as it is. Suppose a curious person should ask the question. It is as an answer to him that the *ṛṣi* says: the *puruṣa* in the beginning did try to get at food with all his faculties, but failed except when using *apāna*. We, the continuators of that *puruṣa*, are also therefore incapable of satisfying our hunger except by the eating of food.

तत् प्राणेनाजिघृक्षत्, तन्नाशक्नोत् प्राणेन ग्रहीतुम्। स यद्धैनत् प्राणेनाग्रहैष्यदभिप्राण्य हैवान्नमत्रप्स्यत्।। ४ ।।

tat prāṇenājighṛkṣat, tan nāśaknot prāṇena grahītum; sa yad hainat prāṇenāgrahaiṣyad abhiprāṇya haivānnam atrapsyat ।। 4 ।।

The *puruṣa* sought to seize food by means of his *prāṇa*, but found himself unable to do so. Had he taken hold of it by *prāṇa*, man would have had his satisfaction just by smelling food.

तच्चक्षुषाजिघृक्षत्, तन्नाशक्नोच्चक्षुषा ग्रहीतुम्। स यद्धैनच्चक्षुषाग्रहैष्यद् दृष्ट्वा हैवान्नमत्रप्स्यत्।। ५ ।।

tac cakṣuṣājighṛkṣat, tan nāśaknoc cakśuṣā grahītum, sa yad hainac cakṣusāgrahaiṣyad dṛṣṭvā haivānnam atrapsyat ।। 5 ।।

The *puruṣa* sought to seize food by means of his sight, but found himself unable to do so. Had he taken hold of it by his eyes, man would have had satisfaction just by seeing food.

तच्छ्रोत्रेणाजिघृक्षत्, तन्नाशक्नोच्छ्रोत्रेण ग्रहीतुम्। स यद्धैनच्छ्रोत्रेणाग्रहैष्यच्छ्रुत्वा हैवान्नमत्रप्स्यत्।। ६ ।।

tac chrotreṇājighṛkṣat, tan nāśaknoc chrotreṇa grahītum; sa yad hainac chrotreṇāgrahaiṣyac chrutvā haivānnam atrapsyat ।। 6 ।।

The *puruṣa* sought to seize food by means of his hearing, but found himself unable to do so. Had he taken hold of it by his ears, man would have had satisfaction just by the hearing of food.

तत्त्वचाजिघृक्षत्, तन्नाशक्नोत्त्वचा ग्रहीतुम्। स यद्धैनत्त्वचाग्रहैष्यत्स्पृष्ट्वा हैवान्नमत्रप्स्यत्।। ७ ।।

tat tvacājighṛkṣat, tan nāśaknot tvacā grahītum; sa yad hainat tvacāgrahaiṣyat spṛṣṭvā haivānnam atrapsyat ।। 7 ।।

The *puruṣa* sought to seize food by means of his skin, but found himself unable to do so. Had he taken hold of it by his skin he would have had satisfaction just by touching food.

तन्मनसाजिघृक्षत्, तन्नाशक्नोन्मनसा ग्रहीतुम्। स यद्धैनन्मनसाग्रहैष्यद्, ध्यात्वा हैवान्नमत्रप्स्यत्।। ८ ।।

tan manasājighṛkṣat, tan nāśaknon manasā grahītum; sa yad hainan mansāgrahaiṣyad dhyātvā haivānnam atrapsyat ।। 8 ।।

The *puruṣa* sought to seize food by means of his mind, but found himself unable to do so. Had he taken hold of it by his mind, he would have attained satisfaction just by thinking of food.

तच्छिश्नेनाजिघृक्षत्, तन्नाशक्नोच्छिश्नेन ग्रहीतुम्। स यद्धैनच्छिश्नेनाग्रहैष्यद्विसृज्य हैवान्नमत्रप्स्यत्।। ९ ।।

tac chiśnenājighṛkṣat, tan nāśaknoc chiśnena grahītum; sa yad hainac chiśnenāgrahaiṣyad visṛjya haivānnam atrapsyat ।। 9 ।।

The *puruṣa* sought to seize food by means of his sex organs, but found himself unable to do so. Had he taken hold of it by his sex organs man would have had satisfied his hunger for food just by emission.

तदपानेनाजिघृक्षत्, तदावयत्। सैषोऽन्नस्य ग्रहो यद्वायुरन्नायुर्वा एष यद्वायुः ।। १० ।।

tad apanenājighṛkṣat, tad āvayat, saiṣo'nnasya graho yad vāyur annāyur vā eṣa yad vāyuḥ ।। 10 ।।

The *puruṣa* then sought to seize food by means of *apāna*. He did seize it, for *apāna* is the air that grasps food. This *apāna* is that sustains life with food.

All other faculties finding themselves incapable of imbibing food, *apāna* alone accomplishes it. *Apāna* is the faculty that found the navel, the central vital point of the human body, which is also the point physically connected to ones's mother, and also the focal area of the digestive action, as its abode. Also *apāna* is the individuated aspect of the cosmic phenomenon death, conceived so because the function of *apāna* results in the death of food, as already observed. Life-sustenance, in other words, relies on the death of food, so this is how *apāna* is death individuated, as the *ṛṣi* perceives it. *Apāna* thus gains a new status in the *ṛṣi*'s vision: that of *annāyuḥ*, the sustainer of life with food.

The *apāna* and its function conceived of here is very different from the *apāna* concept of some other Upaniṣads and some other disciplines. As held by *Āyurveda*, the Indian school of medicine, for example, the digestive function is performed by *prāṇa*, *apāna*'s function being to excrete. When a *ṛṣi*, who is a visionary, intuitively perceives a life system, the technical terms he makes use of may have a sense of their own, sometimes at variance with the prevailing notions. A *ṛṣi* is a seer. His intention is not that of presenting a philosophy of life that agrees with all the prevailing ideas and disciplines. Going into as much details as possible without sacrificing the integrity and structural coherence of the overall vision, will be the *ṛṣi*'s main concern. Any attempt on our part to get into that vision and to make it our own, should, therefore, not be guided by definitions and notions conceived by other thinkers and schools. Rather, we should get enlightened onto the realm of vision the *ṛṣi* was in when he wrote those words, and directly experience the integrity of vision for ourselves, by ourselves. That the present concept of *apāna* and its function, is not in line with any of the prevailing schools of thought or discipline, does in no way therefore discredit the *ṛṣi*'s vision.

स ईक्षत कथं न्विदं मदृते स्यादिति। स ईक्षत कतरेण प्रपद्या इति। स ईक्षत यदि वाचाभिव्याहृतं, यदि प्राणेनाभिप्राणितं, यदि चक्षुषा दृष्टं, यदि श्रोत्रेण श्रुतं, यदि त्वचा स्पृष्टं, यदि मनसा ध्यातं, यद्यपानेनाभ्यपानितं, यदि शिश्नेन विसृष्टमथ कोऽहमिति।। ११ ।।

sa īkṣata: katham nvidam mad ṛte syād iti. sa īksata katareṇa prapadyā iti. sa īkṣata, yadi vācābhivyāhṛtam; yadi prāṇenābhiprāṇitam, yadi cakṣuṣā dṛṣṭam, yadi śrotreṇa śrutam, yadi tvacā spṛṣṭam, yadi manasā dhyātam, yady apānenābhyapānitam, yadi śiśnena visṛṣṭam, atha ko'ham iti ॥ 11 ॥

He (*ātmā*) thought: How can this (the world thus created) exist without me? He thought again: By which of the two openings shall I enter the beings (individual *puruṣa*s)? He thought (again): If speech can articulate on its own, if *prāṇa* can breathe on its own, if eyes can see on their own, if ears can hear on their own, if skin can feel on its own, if mind can think on its own, if *apāna* can digest food on its own, if sex organs can emit on their own, then who am I?

How the food that was getting away was got at by the individual *puruṣa* by means of his *apāna*, was seen in the last stanza. How did *apāna* acquire this capability? Likewise, how did speech acquire the ability to articulate, *prāṇa* to breathe, eyes to see, ears to hear, and so on? How did each of the faculties of each living being acquire their particular capability? The answer is revealed in the present stanza as well as in the ones to come.

The *ṛṣi*, intending to make the revelation, sets a dramatic scene: *Ātmā*, the Creator, looks at the worlds He created from Himself and sees them functioning as though on their own. He thinks: If they can function on their own, then who am I? How can the inert body, sense-organs, and other faculties engage in their respective activities without My presence in them? They remain active, He knows, only because of His presence in them. They and the individual *puruṣas* are seemingly unaware of this reality. They need to be made aware of it. *Ātmā* therefore decides to enter the individual *puruṣas*, where He faces yet another problem: Which way to enter? Two possible ways of entering are there, to be made explicit later. Of the two, *ātmā* chose to enter the *puruṣa* rather than entering his various faculties separately. He made an opening at the crown of the *puruṣa*'s head, and entered his being as will be shown in the next stanza.

Many are the upaniṣadic references which conceive of *ātmā* or *Brahman* as the Eye of eyes, the Ear of ears, the Mind of minds, the *prāṇa* of *prāṇas*, and so on; particularly in the *Kena Upaniṣad* (I.2). Though suggesting the same idea, the picture portrayed here is a somewhat twisted one. All the worlds and all the beings in them including man, emerged from one *ātmā* as a result of His *tapas* or self-heating up. The very same *ātmā* then looks at all of them to see for Himself how they manage as living entities. That He alone is the one Reality that fills the being of all of them, is, in all probability, fully known to *ātmā*. Only the worldly phenomena that emerged from *ātmā*, including man, and his faculties, exist and function seemingly unaware of it. They look as though they are living, thinking of themselves as independent beings. Ignorant as he is of the one Reality that assumes the form of his being, man needs enlightening. *Ātmā* facing the problems is a mere literary device conceived by the *ṛṣi* to enlighten man, who lives unaware of the *ātmā* in himself. *Ātmā* therefore decides to enter man with his knowledge.

Seeing his own bodily and mental faculties in action, man may sometimes ask himself: Do they function on their own? He realises then that his own existence, the existence of all his faculties and their functions, are all here because of the existence of a consciousness that plans, a Reality that plans. Yet he feels, he, in his day to day life, is unaware of that Reality. He therefore feels the necessity to give proper place to that one Reality in his understanding of himself. *Ātmā*, that one Reality, heretofore was either unknown to him or alien to him.

This craving of man to know *ātmā* is what is dramtically portrayed here as *ātmā* deciding to enter the *puruṣa*. But, man asks himself:

Which is the way *ātmā* is to be allowed in? He sees no such way, for to know *ātmā* as the one real substance in oneself is unlike all other kinds of knowledge. So its way of knowing must also be different.

That *ātmā*, after creating the world and beings from Himself, entered all of them, is a concept very dear to many Upaniṣads. Really, no such re-entry of *ātmā* is warranted. To say that clay, after getting transformed pots and other utensils, entered the very same objects is meaningless; to conceive that gold, after becoming ornaments, entered them is also senseless. Equally meaningless is to think of *ātmā* as entering the world that emerged from Itself, for *ātmā* Itself is the Reality in all the appearances. Yet such an entry takes place in man's perception of the world and of himself. Ignorant as he is, man thinks of himself as an entity existing on its own; his faculties as functioning on their own, completely oblivious of the one substance, *ātmā*, that underlies all. His understanding requires a transformation, letting in *ātmā* into the bering of all. The re-entry of *ātmā* into the beings mentioned here, therefore, is not to be construed as a miraculous act performed by *ātmā*, the Creator, after creating the world. Rather it shows man becoming willing, equally miraculous, to see the beingness of *ātmā* in the being of everything. Symbolic of this transformation in man's understanding is the dramatic moment devised here by the *r̥ṣi*.

Feeling how imperative it is to allow *ātmā* in, man begins to think of a way to achieve it, the Upaniṣad portraying it as *ātmā*'s search for an opening to enter the *puruṣa*. The word *katareṇa* (which one of the two) shows that two possibilities were open to It. One is that of entering the *puruṣa*'s being, stated in the next stanza, but what the other way is not mentioned, leaving it to the student to surmise. The main problem introduced was: if speech, *prāṇa*, sight, hearing, and other faculties could function on their own, what would then be the *ātmā*'s role? The real underlying substance and life force in all these faculties, *ātmā* can either enter them separately and make them alive, or enter the whole being of the *puruṣa*, thus enlivening all the faculties together. The latter accords with the creation picture so far depicted. Cosmologically perceived, it would mean *ātmā* entering the cosmic *puruṣa* or the cosmic system, keeping each and every part of it alive. Diametrically opposed is the idea that *ātmā* can separately enter each and every being in the cosmos, as also into each of the faculties of man.

It would result in the cosmos remaining in an incoherent chaotic state, and in the faculties of man not forming part of a coherent human being. *Ātmā* therefore chose the other way. Its entering the *puruṣa*, indidvidual or cosmic, is, in other words, of a vertical order, rather than of a horizontally spread out one, suggested more clearly by the act of piercing a hole in the crown of man's head to enter the body. How unique is the knowledge by which one perceives the entire cosmos as held together by the one all-abiding *ātmā*, is implied in the dramatic entry of *ātmā*.

स एतमेव सीमानं विदार्यैतया द्वारा प्रापद्यत। सैषा विदृतिर्नाम द्वास्तदेतन्नान्दनम्।

तस्य त्रय आवसथाः त्रयः स्वप्नाः। अयमावसथोऽयमावसथोऽयमावसथ इति।। १२ ।।

sa etam eva sīmānaṁ vidāryaitayā dvārā prāpadyata, saiṣā vidṛtir nāma dvāḥ, tad etan nāndanam; tasya traya āvasathās trayaḥ svapnāḥ, ayam āvasatho'yam āvasatho'yam āvasatha iti ।। 12 ।।

Ātmā, piercing a hole at the crown of the *puruṣa*'s head, entered his being thus. That is the hole well-known as *vidṛti*, the seat of rapture. He, having thus entered, found three abodes within, with three respective dreams, referrable as: 'This is my abode', 'This is my abode', 'This is my abode'.

How *ātmā* entered the *puruṣa*'s being and how It found Its abode in the three alternating states of consciousness of the *puruṣa*, is the theme meditated on in this stanza.

What *ātmā* entering the *puruṣa* means, we have already seen. The way *ātmā* chose to enter was the hole named *vidṛti* at the crown of the head of man. Such an opening in the skull does physically exist in new-born babies, which later gets closed with the growth of the skull-bone. Though conscious, a new-born baby has no conscious functions. As the ability to function consciously develops, the hole in the skull gets closed. This biological fact also might have induced the *ṛṣi* to perceive that *ātmā* entered the *puruṣa* through the *vidṛti* opening and found three alternating abodes within: the three states of consciousness. *Vidṛti* could then be taken to symbolically stand for the *turīya* (the fourth), the transcendental experience of non-dual bliss, effectively introduced by treating it as the seat of rapture. A mythological concept that *ātmā* enters the human body through the *vidṛti* at the time of birth and leaves it at death through the same hole, also obtains. It is through this hole, according to the Indian school of medicine, that the coolness of the oil applied to the head penetrates into the skull. The word *vidṛti* means, that which is cut open.

Vidṛti, being such, is treated here as the seat of *ānanda*. *Ānanda* (value experience) is what makes life meaningful. Though a conscious experience, *ānanda* is not counted as a mere function of consciousness (*cit*) by the *ṛṣis*. Instead, *ātmā* is itself *ānanda* in essence, along with being, *cit* (consciousness), also in essence, we remaining ignorant of this notwithstanding. *Ānanda* unconditioned is experienced as *turīya*, literally the fourth, the ineffable experience of non-dual beingness, symbolised here by *vidṛti*. Conditioned by the *puruṣa*, by the human conditions of the altering states of consciousness, *ānanda* assumes various forms of pleasures and pains of the varying states — these three states being *jāgarita* (waking), *svapna* (dreaming), and *suṣupti* (deep sleep). When in one state, the others seem to be non-existent. Being in one state and having its pleasures and pains only is possible at any particular point of time, though the three conditioning states constantly alternate. Such conditioned experience of the *ānanda* content of oneself is actualisable only when the *cit* and *sat* contents of *ātmā* become conditioned by the individuating factors and appear as a living organism, denoted by the word *jīva* in Sanskrit. It becoming possible is symbolically and poetically conceived as *ātmā* entering the *puruṣa* through one's *vidṛti*. Unconditioned, *ānanda* is one. Conditioned, it appears as many, symbolised by *ātmā*, on entering the *puruṣa*, finding different abodes for itself within.

The rapture or supreme blissfulness (*ānanda*) implied in the word *nāndanam*, literally that which relates to rapture, rendered here as 'the seat of rapture', is not simply the highest pleasure all the pleasure-seekers are after. What we consider as pleasure is only one of the conditioned manifestations of the unconditioned *ānanda*, pain being another. *Ānanda* is thus the common value factor in both pleasure and pain; it is the changeless norm by which we evaluate every experience as pleasurable or painful.

Ātmā entering into the individual renders the *puruṣa* fully alive and It becomes able to feel the pleasures and pains in all the states. The activities of a fully alive individual being take place in its various states of consciousness, alternating between the wide awake state and unconscious deep sleep. Consciousness at the former extreme functions as the subject who knows and enjoys all the gross external objects. At the other extreme, consciousness goes back to its functionless seed-like state, experienced by us as the unconscious blissfulness of deep sound sleep. The former is known as *jāgarita* and the latter *suṣupti*. In between these two extremities come numerous other states. A middle one, named *svapna* (dreaming) is also often conceived of for convenience sake. What is peculiar to the dreaming state is that a world of its own is created by the dreaming mind, which the very same mind enjoys as though it is a gross material world. Nevertheless, no strict compartmentalisation of the functions of consciousness is practically possible, for no one knows when one drifts from one state to the other. We could rather say that consciousness in its ceaseless onward flow oscillates between full wakefulness and the unconsiousness of deep sleep. Anyway, the three abodes *ātmā* found in the *puruṣa*'s being should be the above mentioned *jagarita*, *svapna*, and *suṣupti*.

A dreaming mind, as we have just seen, is such that it creates a world within itself and enjoys this very same world. All the worlds, according to the present creation story, emerge from one *ātmā*, and this same *ātmā*, entering them, enjoys them. So *ātmā* is a dreaming mind, the dream-world and all the pleasures and pains having no existence apart from that mind. What we saw as the three alternating states of consciousness — *jāgarita*, *svapna*, and *suṣupti* — are nothing but part of the grand dream dreamed by one *ātmā*, nothing more than three different dreams dreamed by *ātmā* while within the *puruṣa*.

The dream-happenings continue to be felt as real until and unless the dreamer wakes up. Once awake, all the dream-appearances disappear in the dreamer, he alone remaining. *Ātmā*, likewise, dreams the worlds, and their existence is only in His dream, as his dream. All of them, on *ātmā*'s waking up, disappear in *ātmā*, *ātmā* alone remaining.

Narayana Guru in his *Advaita Dīpikā* (The Lamp of Non-duality) clarifies this point thus:

> The world, unless pondered on properly, is real;
> Dream-sights, until the dreamer's waking up, seem real,
> On his waking up, they *in toto* merge in him.

स जातो भूतान्यभिव्यैख्यत् किमिहान्यं वावदिषदिति। स एतमेव पुरुषं ब्रह्म ततममपश्यदिदमदर्शमिती।। १३ ।।

sa jāto bhūtany abhivyaikhyat kim ihānyaṁ vāvadiṣad iti, sa etam eva puruṣaṁ brahma tatamam apaśyad, idam ādarśam iti ।। 13 ।।

The one who thus took birth, looked at the born beings one by one and observed:

'What is here to be spoken of as 'the other'?'
He perceived the all-pervading
Brahman in the very same *puruṣa*.
He exlaimed: 'Now I see it!'

'Really who am I?' This question arises in certain human beings, and that too very rarely. Mostly we remain unaware that what took birth as our being is *ātmā*, the one all-pervading Reality. Everyone thus remains ignorant of oneself while seemingly living as oneself. *Ātmā* entering the *puruṣa* as portrayed in the last stanza could well be considered as symbolising man's becoming aware of the *ātmā*-reality in himself, similar to the concept of the Holy spirit entering Jesus as a pigeon as he was being baptised by John the Baptist. The one who thus becomes aware of himself is a *jñānin*. He sees himself as one of the countless specific forms in which the one Reality (*ātmā*) manifests. A man of such wisdom is the one referred to here as '*saḥ jātaḥ*' (the one who thus took birth).

The one who sees himself as *ātmā* embodied will see others also in exactly the same light. All being thus one in essence, nothing will be seen by him to be spoken of as 'the other'. He sees *ātmā* alone in all beings. *Ātmā* meaning oneself, he sees himself alone in all beings.

Ātmā means also the substance that underlies one's own beingness. The same substance that underlies all beings in all the worlds, is called *Brahman*, literally that which constantly grows. One who sees oneself as *ātmā*, he sees himself as *Brahman* in essence also, as he sees *Brahman* alone in all beings. Aspiring towards such a vision of oneness, the supplicant of the *Īśa Upaniṣad* prays God or *Brahman*:

> O Pūṣan, the lone seer, please subdue your effulgence so that I may directly perceive the most auspicious being of yours. That imperceptible being, perceived as everything here, is itself the being in me.

The *puruṣa*'s visualising one *ātmā*—of whom he was born—in himself, as the substance of his own beingness, comes to its finale with this stanza. He sees himself as *Brahman*, and this makes him exclaim, 'Now I see It!'

तस्मादिदन्द्रो नामेदन्द्रो ह वै नाम। तमिदन्द्रं सन्तमिन्द्र इत्याचक्षते परोक्षेण।
परोक्षप्रिया इव हि देवाः, परोक्षप्रिया इव हि देवाः।। १४ ।।

tasmād idandro nāmedandro ha vai nāma tam idandraṁ
santam indra ity ācakṣate parokṣeṇa, parokṣa-priyā iva
hi devāḥ parokṣa-priyā iva hi devāḥ || 14 ||

Hence the name Idandra. Idandra indeed is a well-known name. Idandra the good, is indirectly spoken of as Indra, for Gods seemingly are fond of what is indirect. Gods seemingly are fond of what is indirect.

A visionary who perceives *Brahman* alone in each and every specific entity, and who exclaims, 'Now I see it!' is given the name Idandra. Literally, it means, one who runs up to whatever can be referred to as 'this' (*idam*). What one sees then is the multiplicity of reality. Looking at reality this-wise is direct perception, called *pratyakṣa*. The one substance underlying every 'this' could also be perceived, but it would be an indirect (*parokṣa*) perception. Good and evil are meaningful considerations only when multiplicity is perceived as real. Indirectly perceiving the one Reality in all the directly perceptible multiple entities, one becomes free from the good-evil duality, reaching a state of absolute goodness. Idandra in that sense is considered *sat* (good) here.

Vedānta, we know, is a continuation of the Vedas, while being a revision and revaluation of them. What is important in the Vedas is praising Gods in heaven and offering oblations to them while praying for their favours. The chief of all such gods is Indra. His chiefhood is accommodated into the Vedāntic context of wisdom, by equating him with Idandra, a clear instance of how Vedānta corrects Vedism without rejecting it.

Gods of heaven get pleasure not by enjoying objects directly, but by indirectly enjoying them as oblations offered by human beings. Gods thus are the enjoyers of the indirect, and Indra is their chief. His Vedic love for the indirect objects, when subjected to the Vedāntic revision, becomes Idandra's love for the indirectly perceptible *Brahman*.

To consider sense organs as *devas* (gods) is customary among Indian seers, which at the beginning of this creation story, was found reflected when considering human faculties as divinities (*devatās*). The word *deva* means 'the shinning one'. Different outlets of knowledge, sense organs are effulgence in essence, and to that extent are *devas*. Though what one experiences as a result of sense contact is sense perception, it is nothing but a particular way in which the consciousness-content of our being shines; and thus, a manifestation of *Brahman*. Sense perception, thus, helps a seeker perceive *Brahman* indirectly. Among such indirect perceivers of *Brahman*, Indra is the chief, which status, is given recognition to in other Upaniṣads also. The *Kena Upaniṣad* for instance, in a similar context, says, 'For this reason, Indra is above all other gods'.

A prayer addressed to Indra in the *Taittirīya Upaniṣad* says: 'Indra, being such, may enlighten me with proper intelligence'.

PART II

Section One

[अपक्रामत(न्तु) गर्भिण्यः] पुरुषे ह वा अयमादितो गर्भो भवति यदेतद्रेतः।
तदेतत्सर्वेभ्योऽङ्गेभ्यस्तेजः सम्भूतमात्मन्येवात्मानं बिभर्ति; तद्यदा स्त्रियां
सिञ्चत्यथैनज्जनयति; तदस्य प्रथमं जन्म।। १ ।।

puruṣe ha vā ayam ādito garbho bavati, yad etad retas tad etat sarvebhyo'ṅgebhyas tejaḥ sambhūtam, ātmany evātmānaṁ bibharti, tad yathā striyāṁ siñcati athainaj janayati, tad asya prathamaṁ janma ।। 1 ।।

This one becomes the first pregnancy in man: the semen he carries. The vigour drawn out as it is from all the limbs, it conserves oneself in the self. Depositing it in a woman, one is giving birth to it. Of *ātmā*, this event is the first birth.

तत् स्त्रिया आत्मभूयं गच्छति, यथा स्वमङ्गं तथा; तस्मादेनां न हिनस्ति;
सास्यैतमात्मानमत्र गतं भावयति।। २ ।।

tat striyā ātmabhūyaṁ gacchati, yathā svam aṅgam tathā, tasmād enāṁ na hinasti, sāsyaitam ātmānam atra gataṁ bhāvayati ।। 2 ।।

It (man's self-essence thus deposited) attains selfhood in the woman, as if a limb of hers. It therefore does not hurt her. She nurtures that self of him that became hers.

सा भावयित्री भावयितव्या भवति। तं स्त्री गर्भं बिभर्ति। सोऽग्र एव कुमारं जन्मनोऽग्रेऽधिभावयति। स यत् कुमारं जन्मनोऽग्रेऽधिभावयति, आत्मानमेव तद्भावयति, एषां लोकानां सन्तत्या। एवं सन्तता हीमे लोकास्तदस्य द्वितीयं जन्म।। ३ ।।

sā bhāvayatrī bhāvayitavyā bhavati, taṁ strī garbhaṁ vibharti । *so'gra eva kumāraṁ janmano'gre'dhi bhāvayati. sa yat kumāraṁ janmano'gre'dhibhāvayati ātmānam eva tad bhāvayati eṣāṁ lokānāṁ saṁtatya* । *evaṁ saṁtatā hīme lokāḥ, tad asya dvitīyaṁ janma* ।। 3 ।।

Nurturer, she is to be nurtured. The woman thus carries securely that embryo within, and he (the husband) takes care of the child before and after delivery. His taking care of the child before and after delivery, in essence, is his taking care of himself for the continuance of the world of progeny. Indeed, thuswise the world of progeny continues. Of *ātmā*, this event is the second birth.

सोऽस्यायमात्मा पुण्येभ्यः कर्मभ्यः प्रतिधीयते। अथास्यायमितर आत्मा कृतकृत्यो वयोगतः प्रैति। स इतः प्रयन्नेव पुनर्जायते; तदस्य तृतीयं जन्म।। ४ ।।

so'syāyam ātmā puṇyebhyaḥ karmabhyah pratidhīyate, athāsyāyam itara ātmā kṛta-kṛtyo vayo-gataḥ praiti । *sa itaḥ prayann eva punar jāyate, tad asya tṛtīyaṁ janma* ।। 4 ।।

The son, being such a self of the father, is made a substitute for performance of meritorious deeds. His (father's) other self (himself), thus feeling the self-satisfaction of having fulfilled his duties, and reaching old-age, he departs. By the very departing from here, he is being born again. Of *ātmā*, this event of departing is the third birth.

तदुक्तमृषिणा —
गर्भे नु सन्नन्वेषामवेदमहं देवानां जनिमानि विश्वा। शतं मा पुर आयसीररक्षन्नधः श्येनो जवसा निरदीयमिति। गर्भ एवैतच्छयानो वामदेव एवमुवाच।। ५ ।।

tad uktam ṛṣīṇā —

garbhe nu sann anveṣām avedam ahaṁ devānām janimāni viśvā,
śatam mā pura āyasīr arakṣann adhaḥ śyeno javasā niradīyam
iti, garbha evaitac chayāṇo vāmadeva evam uvāca ।। 5 ।।

It has been stated by the *ṛṣi* thus: While in the womb, I knew all the births of the shining ones one by one. A hundred steel like strongholds were holding me down. But, eagle-like, I came out bursting forth. Thus was declared by Vāmadeva while yet in womb.

स एवं विद्वानस्माच्छरीरभेदादूर्ध्वं उत्क्रम्यामुष्मिन् स्वर्गे लोके सर्वान् कामानाप्त्वाऽमृतः समभवत्ः समभवत् ।। ६ ।।

sa evaṁ vidvān asmāc charīra-bhedād ūrdhvaṁ utkramy-āmuṣmin svarge loke sarvān kāmān āptvāmṛtaḥ samabhavat, samabhavat ।। 6 ।।

He, knowing thus, going upwards beyond the differences caused by perishing bodies, and attaining all the desirables of life, became immortal in that world of heaven, became immortal indeed!

How the one *ātmā*, by its own will, unfolds itself as this world with a perfect structural coherence and integrity, is what was delineated in the first chapter of the present Upaniṣad. Finally, *ātmā*, visualises its own existence in all the variegated beings thus manifested. What is already drawn thus is the creation picture in its most generic aspect. At the outer periphery of this picture comes every individual living being, man one among them. The same creative self-unfoldment, forced by the same urge from within, continues also through each individual being in the form of procreation. In this process, an individual *puruṣa* undergoes three different stages of being born. This second chapter portrays that picture, yet the basic stand that it is one immortal *ātmā* that underlies all such apparent transformations is not lost sight of. Each individual *puruṣa*, through the process of sexual reproduction, begets new individual *puruṣas*, *ātmā* still remaining immortal.

It Conserves Oneself

An unbroken process, life continues through procreation. To be in a womb, to be born, the born being becoming pregnant with the potential to beget, and giving birth to the new generation — this is the sequential order of the procreative process. It is in view of this sequence that the present chapter of the Upaniṣad visualises the continuance of human progeny, along with man's handing down his duties to the next generation.

The seed of the next generation that abides in his being is never thought of or felt by man as an 'other' entity, nor does he feel that he conserves something within. It simply remains an unidentifiable part of his beingness. The only feeling he has will be of his being conserved by himself, or self conserving itself. So it is said, 'It conserves oneself in the self' (*ātmani eva ātmānam bibharti*).

Many Births

The seed man is already pregnant with, is first deposited into the womb of a woman through their sexual union, which event is here considered the first birth of the man's self-being or *puruṣa*. Considering so, a wont not very common, signifies that the many births mentioned in this chapter are not meant to be understood as a series of ordinary births of a human being, held by believers in the popular notion of reincarnation. It could even be counted as a subtle way of correcting it. Something latent gets developed and becomes apparent. The former state is called cause, and the latter, effect. The causal state is like pregnancy; while the appearance of the effect, in effect, is its birth. The series of births conceived here signifies this long line of cause-effect relationship that sustains reproduction, every new effect the cause of yet another new effect. The seed pregnant in man, born thus, assumes a new pregnant state, this time the women's ordinary pregnancy. When time is ripe happens yet another birth — the actual birth of the child — which is the second birth of the *puruṣa*. Just as the seed remained inseparable in man's beingness, the newly formed embryo also remains in the woman one with her, she not having the feeling of carrying something 'else'. What this oneness signifies is this: Effect, latent in cause, has no existence apart from cause.

Self-Nurturing

A pregnant woman protects the embryo in her with the feeling that she protects herself. That, that woman also in her turn needs protection and nurturing is not only a generally accepted social convention, it also is an inborn need a husband feels within himself. By nurturing the wife who is carrying a bit of his own being, he virtually is nurturing his self. Rearing the child properly, is likewise, not only the social responsibility of a father but also an imperative he feels within, child, for a father, is not another being, it is merely an extension of himself. Helping it attain perfection means helping himself attain perfection. Through it he is ensuring the immortal existence of his own being, which in effect is actualising thc immortality of life in the world. Such is the creative urge in the self — *ātmā* or *puruṣa* — to sustain itself, to sustain life.

Death is Birth

The next scene of birth is that a father leaving this world after making his son — his own self attained perfection — his representative in performing all the good deeds he was doing. The preservation of the world and its constant creative self-unfoldment requires that each individual being, that is part of it, be engaged in activities natural to them. Individual beings appear and disappear, but the creative self-unfoldment — that which we call *karma* — continues unceasing. Each newly emerging individual takes on the *karma* of his predecessor, if possible in a better way. Part of this is a father's leaving this world after entrusting his son with his responsibilities to the family, to the world, and to gods, with a sense of satisfaction in seeing himself continuing in spite of his disappearance. Such a disappearance of man — what we call death — is what is counted here as the third birth of the *puruṣa*.

Treating what we know as death, as birth may sound paradoxical. It looks so only because we are oblivious of the fact that it is the disappearance of an existing form that emerges as the apearance of a new one. What really exists is the one unborn, deathless *ātmā*. Only apparent forms are born; only they can die. It is the death of something or certain things that assumes the form of the birth of a new thing. An egg, for example, when hatched, becomes a chick. The event of the birth of the chick is also the event of the death of the egg. This fact, in our usual course of life, is not noticed, only because what dies in the birth of a body is not one single entity alone, but numerous elements together in a complex state. The event of the birth of a chick in fact, for example, is also a complex one. It is not the egg alone that is destroyed or consumed; the warmth and moisture absorbed from the mother-hen, the atmosphere, air, and moisture constituted of numerous elements, and many other factors were consumed by the egg before getting hatched. Really it is the death of all those factors together that became the birth of the chick. What is of concern here is not, what happens to the individual at his death. That, every disappearance of something is the appearance of something else, is what matters, for this ensures the ceaseless continuation of life. It is not stated here in the Upaniṣad that the dead one, departing from here, is reborn in a new body somewhere else. Death, on the other hand, itself becomes the third birth of man, as is underscored in the words, 'By the very departing from here, he is being born again (*sa itaḥ prayann eva punar-jāyate*).

What is born in this third birth, i.e., in man's death, also should be a causal state of something new, or many new causal states of many new things, of some new pregnancy as in the case of the two previous births. The nature of that embryonic being or beings is beyond the grasp of our mind. It is as equally mysterious as *ātmā* going to the seed-like pregnant state in man's semen. The known factors of life and the unknown mysterious factors, in short, embracing and becoming inseparably one, ensure the continuance of life in a pregnancy-birth-pregnancy-birth sequence.

Vāmadeva's Story

The *r̥ṣi* Vāmadeva's story is cited to back up the vision of life depicted so far. He is a Vedic *r̥ṣi* well-known as the author of the fourth part of the *Ṛgveda* as well as for attaining his immortality even as he was in his mother's womb. He, in the words quoted, says, he knew thuswise the secret of the birth of all the *devas*. How birth and being in womb are related — every birth being a new pregnant state and every new pregnant state being a new birth — we have already seen. Even as all such unceasing transformations occur, the one Substance *ātmā*, in which they take place, remains unchanging and eternal. It is immortal. Perceiving the immortal Reality and the always changing transient appearances, in their inseparable oneness, one not existing without the other, is the secret knowledge about the shining ones. Vāmadeva, being a *ṛṣi* of the Vedas, the *devas* he knew were also of the same context. This legend is given a revised Vedāntic meaning here in the Upaniṣad — by treating the knowledge of the birth of gods as the knowledge of the birth and being in womb of all beings. *Ātmā* is effulgence in essence. Whatever form *ātmā* assumes in its ceaseless creative self-unfoldment, is a different form of the same effulgence, a different god or shining one. Perceiving every transient appearence as a different manifestation of the one eternal *ātmā*, effulgence in essence, thus becomes the secret knowledge of the birth of all the shining ones.

To be in womb and to be born, are two aspects of the existence of every indidvidual being, as part of the eternal flow of the *karma* of Nature. Both states have one thing in common: they are bodily bound. Getting rid of that bondage is a delicate job, and no easy one. Giving up that bondage, in one sense, means negating our own existence as actual living beings. Such being the strong bondage all living beings are in, it is compared to a hundred steel chains holding one down. So long as this bondage exists, our understanding of ourselves will be relative to it, conditioned by it; it will never be the absolute knowledge, the unconditioned knowledge. Yet it is possible to see ourselves as the eternal Reality, to free ourselves from the bondage. Each individual seeing himself as a particular form in which one eternal *ātmā* become manifest, comparable to a gold ornament seeing itself as one of the many transient forms of the eternal gold, is the way it is accomplished. Only this awareness, this enlightenment, enables one to shatter the steel chains and make oneself free of all the bodily bondage. This liberatedness is compared here to an eagle soaring high in the sky. Experiencing thus liberated, Vāmadeva, still in womb, saw that, whatever form a being is in, whether as an embryo or as a born being, is a particular kind of being in womb. Every such state is a state of being bodily bound. Liberation and bondage, both are meaningful only when existing bodily; both are experienceable only when existing bodily. A bodiless state is simply an unknown, unthinkable, indistinct one, hidden behind the dark screen of unknowability; neither understandable nor experienceable.

The legend holds that the *ṛṣi* Vāmadeva got liberated and attained heaven while in womb. By this allusion, the seekers who make use of this Upaniṣad as an aid, are intended to see themselves in the place of the *ṛṣi*. That the heaven he reached is not the Vedic one, is given emphasis to by qualifying it as 'this' (*amuṣmin*).

Attaining all the Desirables

That all desires get fulfilled by learning what is taught therein, is a common promise given in most of the scriptures including the Upaniṣads and the *Bhagavad Gītā*. Trapped by the countless desires as we are, we might misconstrue such scriptural utterances as meaning that by learning those scriptures all one's worldly desires would be fulfilled. We remain oblivious then that it is worldly desires, rather than wisdom, that we are being led by. A real seer, a *jñānin*, sees only one Reality in everything, everywhere. Who, then, desires what? Desire itself then becomes meaningless. Desireless, the attainer of wisdom feels the satisfaction of having fulfilled all desires in life. It is an irony that fulfilling all desires one by one and thus to come to a state of fulfilment is an impossibility, for desires are endless. Fulfilling certain of them creates new ones, needing more efforts, which in turn lead to more desires, all ending up in total frustration. Having no desire at all alone, therefore, is that which gives us the satisfaction of having fulfilled all desires.

PART III

Section One

कोऽयमात्मेति वयमुपास्महे। कतरः स आत्मा येन वा (रूपं) पश्यति, येन
वा (शब्दं) शृणोति, येन वा गन्धानाजिघ्रति, येन वा वाचं व्याकरोति, येन
वा स्वादु चास्वादु च विजानाति।। १ ।।

ko'yam ātmeti vayam upāsmahe, kataraḥ sa ātmā, yena vā paśyati, yena vā śṛṇoti, yena vā gandhān ājighrati, yena vā vācaṁ vyākaroti, yena vā svādu cāśvādu ca vijānāti ।। 1 ।।

'What is it (we are dealing with here)?
'What we meditatively adore as *ātmā*'.
'Of the two, which one is that *ātmā*?'
'That because of which one sees, because of which one hears, because of which one smells odours, because of which one discriminates the flavoured and the flavourless — that indeed is *ātmā*'.

This final chapter depicts what in essence is that which unfolds as everything. This first stanza of it, is differently interpretable: One, by seeing the entire stanza as forming a series of questions: 'What is it we are dealing with here?' 'Of the two, which is that *ātmā*?' 'Is it the *ātmā* we meditate on?' 'Is it that because of which one sees, that because of which one hears, that because of which one smells odours, that because of which one discriminates between the flavoured and the flavourless?' Interpreted differently, the first part ending with, 'Of the two, which is the *ātmā*?' is the question, and the rest the answer. Yet another interpretation possible is, as a series of questions and answers, the one preferred in our translation. The stanza being so, nevertheless, does in no way affect its main point.

The first question is, 'What is it?', meaning, 'What really is it that we are dealing with?' It helps us get at the crux of the teaching. The answer is, 'It is that which we meditate upon as *ātmā*, as oneself, as the Self.'

The *puruṣa* has already perceived what is real in himself and all else as nothing but *Brahman* (see Stanza I.iii.13 above). Yet meditating and intuitively perceiving *Brahman* as such is an impossibility. What is possible is meditating and perceiving that Reality as oneself, as the Self, a stance confirmed by the *Kena Upaniṣad* also when it repreatedly says, '*Brahman* is not anything meditated on or worshipped as 'this' '. (*Kena Upaniṣad* I.5-9). It, instead of being treated as an object of meditation, is to be experienced as the essential content of one's own beingness. It is that one Substance that assumes the form of the being of oneself, as well as the being of each of our specifiable faculties. The Eye, for example, is capable only of seeing objects different from itself; mind is capable only of thinking of something different from itself. They and all similar faculties never see or conceive their own essential substance. To perceive that Reality, the eye has to look at itself, turning inwards, and experience, 'I am That'; mind has to turn inwards and experience itself as a particular configuration of that Substance, as 'I am That'; the seeker himself has to turn inwards and experience himself as that *Brahman* in essence, as 'I am That'. *Brahman* realised is *ātman*; *ātman* realised is *Brahman*. Putting emphasis on this way of realising *Brahman*, it is repeatedly stated here, 'that because of which one sees, that because of which one hears, and so on. . . , that indeed is *ātmā*'. The *Kena Upaniṣad*, in the very same sense, just before it ends, says, 'Meditatable is it as the nearest of all (*tadvanam*)'. Our own essential content is the nearest of all realities for each of us.

Of the two, which is the *ātmā* so realisable? This is the next question. Which the two are, is not clarified in the text, but unless the two are discriminated between, the crux of the teaching of the Upaniṣad may be lost sight of.

The first chapter of the Upaniṣad began with the statement: 'One *ātmā* alone existed in the beginning. All the worlds, their protectors, the cosmic *puruṣa*, cosmic gross elements, individuating faculties and factors, their functions, the individual *puruṣa*, were all perceived as one *ātmā* manifesting in various forms. The same *ātmā*, entering all that is distinguishable, remains their substance as well. Perceived thus, *ātmā* sees itself in all the worlds. The first chapter thus portrayed the cosmic creativity or *karma* of *ātmā*.

The second chapter described how the same creative urge works within each individual being, resulting in procreation — a ceaseless process that alternates between being in womb and being born, every birth becoming a new state of being in womb. *Ātmā* alone continues to exist through this process. *Ātmā*'s creativity, in other words, manifests with two facets: the universal and the particular, macrocosmic and microcosmic, objective and subjective. A search for the Real could also begin from either of these two.

The two facets are mutually exclusive, while being mutually complementary. Stressing any one in the search for the Real, would bias the approach and the resulting realisation. As a precaution against such an eventuality it is asked here, 'Of the two which is the real *ātmā*?' Answering it, the second stanza that follows shows how all the internal faculties of an individual, the subjective world, are one *prajñāna* (Consciousness) in essence. How everything in all the objective worlds, from Brahmā the creator to tiny germ-like beings, are guided by the very same *prajñāna* is made obvious in the stanza that follows. *Ātmā*, Consciousness (*prjnana*) in essence, is thus perceived from two perspectives. Either is neither admitted nor rejected. Instead, both are brought over to the one homogeneous matrix of unconditioned Consciousness (*prajñāna*), which finally is equated to *Brahman*. *Ātmā* or *Brahman* alone appears as objects to be perceived; *ātmā* alone manifests as perceiving subjects; *ātmā* alone manifests as the sensing experience. By getting into contact with objects and experiencing them, what a subject does is to realise the inherent oneness of both. This realised, vanishes altogether the doubt, "which one of the two is *ātmā*?" It is because of this oneness, that a sense perceives its object. Hence the words: 'That because of which one sees' and so on.

यदेतद्धृदयं मनश्चैतत्। संज्ञानमाज्ञानं विज्ञानं प्रज्ञानं मेधा दृष्टिर्धृतिर्मतिर्मनीषा जूतिः स्मृतिः सङ्कल्पः क्रतुरसुः कामो वश इति — सर्वाण्येवैतानि प्रज्ञानस्य नामधेयानि भवन्ति।। २ ।।

yad etad hṛdayaṁ manaś caitat, saṁjñānaṁ ājñānaṁ vijñānaṁ prajñānaṁ medhā dṛṣṭir dhṛtir matir manīṣā jūtiḥ smṛtiḥ saṁkalpaḥ kratur asuḥ kāmo vaśa iti sarvāṇy evaitāni prajñānasya nāmadheyāni bhavanti ॥ 2 ॥

That which is heart is that (*ātmā*).
That which is mind is also that.
Perception, commanding power, comprehensive knowledge, specific knowledge, retentive power, vision, firmness of mind, reflective mind, free thinking, impulse, memory, conception, purposefulness, life, desire, self-restraint — all these are different names of one and the same *prajñāna*.

Countlessly, various and varying are the functions of our mind. All the ideas and ideals, love and hate, all emotions and impulses, imageries and imagination, understandings and vision, knowledge and ignorance, are different modes that one and the same Consciousness assumes, different conditioned· manifestations of the one unconditioned, unmanifest Consciousness or *prajñāna* which in essence *ātmā* is. *Prajñāna* literally means that because of which everything becomes known. The mental states enumerated in the text are merely a few, representative of the vast subjective world. What is going to be done in like manner in the next stanza is to outline such representative ones in the vast objective world. Even subjectivity and objectivity are experiences occurring in one *prajñāna*. That *prajñāna* is *Brahman* (*prajñānam brahma*), one of the great dicta, is with which the Upaniṣad concludes. Whatever state of mind one is in, whatever the variety of the objective world one encounters, one has to see one *ātmā* or *Brahman*, *prajñāna* in essence, in all of them, and find oneself to be that *prajñāna* in essence, existing as *prajñāna*, and living as *prajñāna*. This is the goal a seeker has to attain with the help of the present Upaniṣad.

एष ब्रह्मैष इन्द्र, एष प्रजापतिरेते सर्वे देवा, इमानि च पञ्चमहाभूतानि — पृथिवी वायुराकाश आपो ज्योतीꣳषीत्येतानि, इमानि च क्षुद्रमिश्राणीव बीजानि, इतराणि चेतराणि चाण्डजानि च जारुजानि च, स्वेदजानि चोद्भिज्जानि चाश्वा गावः पुरुषा हस्तिनो, यत्किञ्चेदं प्राणि जङ्गमं च पतत्रि

च यच्च स्थावरं; सर्वं तत् प्रज्ञानेत्रं प्रज्ञाने प्रतिष्ठितं प्रज्ञानेत्रो लोकः, प्रज्ञा प्रतिष्ठा, प्रज्ञानं ब्रह्म ॥ ३ ॥

eṣa brahmaiṣa indra, eṣa prajāpatir ete sarve devā imāni ca pañca mahābhūtāni, pṛthivī vāyur ākāśa āpo jyotīṁṣīty etānīmāni ca kṣudra-miśrāṇīva, bījānītarāṇi cetarāṇi cāṇḍajāni ca jārujāni ca svedajāni codbhijjāni cāśvā gāvaḥ puruṣā hastino yat kiñ cedam prāṇi jaṅgamaṁ ca patatri ca yac ca sthāvaram, sarvaṁ tat prajñā-netram prajñāne pratiṣṭhitam, prajñā-netro lokaḥ prajñā pratiṣṭhā, prajñānam brahma ॥ 3 ॥

That (*prajñāna*) becomes Brahmā; that becomes Indra; that becomes Prajāpati; that becomes all the gods; that becomes these five great elements, namely, earth, air, space, water, and fire; that becomes the smallest beings, and the mixed ones; that becomes all the seeds of one kind or another; that becomes the beings born of eggs, those born of womb, those born of sweat, those born sprouting; that becomes horses, cows, human beings and elephants. To make it short, whatever living beings are here, whether walking, flying, or stationary — all are guided by *prajña*; they are all well-founded in *prajñāna*. The entire world is guided by *prajñāna*. *Prajñāna*, it is on which all is well-founded. *Prajñāna* is *Brahman*.

The vast subjective world was seen in the last stanza as manifestations of the one *prajñāna*, of the one *ātmā*. Here in this stanza is seen the boundless objective world as well-founded in *prajñāna* and well-guided by *prajñāna*. The representative items enumerated here include everything created, movable or immovable. It may be asked, 'Do the beings like Brahmā, Indra, and other Gods really exist, or are they only poetical fantasies?' Before getting the doubt cleared, let us ask, 'Do the world and the entities in it as we perceive here, really exist as they appear to be? Or, is their existence a mere projection?'

We see everything with our eyes impelled by our mind. The colour, size, and such qualities of the objects we directly see depend on the condition of our eyes; our interest in and the nature of what we see depend on our mental condition. When I see a red object, for example, the redness I experience depends on the nature of my eyesight, and the redness you see depends on yours. Whose eyesight is perfect no one knows. Most probably the eyesight of everyone has its own conditionings and to that extent is faulty. Though, denoted by the word 'red', the redness I feel need not necessarily be like the one you feel, as it always remains a subjective experience. Given that my and your experiences are different, which one is right and which one wrong? Or, are both wrong? Anyway, both cannot be right. In fact, each one of us is having an experience of our own, incomparable with anothers. The world I see is different from the one you see, though we use the same words to describe it. The world each of us sees, in other words, is the one in the mind of each: *mano-mayam idam sarvam* (everything here is of the essence of mind). No one really sees the real world. Whatever I see in my mind is real for me; whatever you see in yours is real for you. The real world remains unknown to and unperceived by anyone. Equally unknown is the mystery of life. And the unknown world and the unknown life, are somehow integrally linked. Life, we know, is not controlled by our free will alone, but by some unknown factors as well. Thinking of those unknown factors as forming part of the unknown world is quite natural. The *ṛṣis*, therefore, fancied the existence of many gods existing in the unknown realm called heaven. To think of the unknowable as non-existing is as foolish as denying our own existence because our existence remains a mystery. One underlying Reality common to both the known and unknown realms of life at least has to be admitted. The *ṛṣi* here visualises that Reality as *prajñāna*, pure unconditioned Consciousness, the essential content of *ātmā*. Consciousness in essence, it is aware of all the creative unfoldment that occurs in itself, which it controls. The word *prajñā-netram* can be interpreted in two ways. *Prajñā* means consciousness, and *netram*, eyes; thus *prajñā-netram* means, the eye of consciousness that witnesses all that occurs in the very same *prajñāna*. *Prajñā-netram* also means, 'that which is guided by *prajñā*'.

All the worlds being a mental projection, the one Substance that underlies the worlds must surely be Mind or Consciousness, pure and unconditioned. As the all-underlying Substance, it is called *Brahma*, as the Substance that underlies each entity it is called *ātmā*; as pure, unconditioned Consciousness in essence it is *prajñāna* or *cit*. *Prajñāna* is realisable as one's own essential content, as one's own existence. This realisable *prajñāna* is nothing but a spark of the Consciousness that underlies the whole, that controls the whole, that is denoted by the word *brahman* that a seeker is in search of. The teaching concludes by equating *prajñāna* and *Brahman*. Realising the *prajñāna* in oneself, therefore, in effect, is equal to realising *Brahman*.

Prajñānam brahma is one of the four great dicta (*mahā-vākyas*), short sentences condensing the essential teaching of Vedānta. The other three are *tat tvam asi* (That thou art) of the *Chāndogya Upaniṣad* appended to the *Sāmaveda*, *aham brahma asmi* (I am *Brahman*) of *Bṛhadāraṇyaka Upaniṣad* appended to the *Yajurveda*, and *ayam ātmā brahma* (This self is *Brahman*) of the *Māṇḍūkya Upaniṣad* appended to the *Adharvaveda*. The present Upaniṣad comes as an appendix to the *Ṛgveda*. Each of these dicta could thus be considered the condensation of the wisdom content of the Veda concerned.

Each dictum is in the form of an equation, its two limbs being the generic and specific aspects of one non-dual Reality. These two limbs are like the two sides of a coin. What is real in the coin is the substance in between the two sides. The two limbs of the equation, likewise, denote the two recognisable yet opposite apparent aspects of what Really exists, which is realisable only.

स एतेन प्रज्ञेनात्मनास्माल्लोकादुत्क्रम्यामुष्मिन् स्वर्गे लोके सर्वान् कामानाऽऽप्त्वामृतः समभवत् समभवत्।। ४ ।।

sa etena prajñenātmanāsmāl lokād utkramyāmuṣmin svarge loke sarvān kāmān āptvāmṛtaḥ samabhavat, samabhavat ।। 4 ।।

He (the *ṛṣi* Vāmadeva), with this enlightenment, transcended this world, fulfilled all desires, and did become immortal in that world of Heaven. He did become immortal!

The second chapter ended with a reference to the *ṛṣi* Vāmadeva attaining immortality, an attainment that resulted from an enlightenment, as was indicated by the phrase *saḥ evam vidvān* (He, knowing thus). That the third chapter was a sort of elucidation of that 'knowing this', becomes clear with the phrase *sah etena prajñena* (He with this enlightenment) of this concluding stanza. This enlightenment, as was seen in the last stanza, leads to the realisation, *prajñānam brahma*. The enlightenment in its turn was arrived at by perceiving the one common substance in both the endlessly expansive subjective world and the endlessly expansive objective world. This common substance is none other than *prajñāna*. The dictum *prajñānam brahma* is a verbal symbol of an ineffable experience of oneness, not to be *understood* and described, but to be *realised*. The internal mental functions of what exists, and the external physical functions of what exists were taken advantage of to arrive at this realisation. The two were treated like the two sides of a coin, as already made clear.

One who realises while living one's oneness with the whole, would also have his own personal needs to be fulfilled, like eating food, to ensure existence. The one Reality that provides for all, will also provide for the needs of the one who lives at one with that Reality. He does not have to ask for it; he does not have to strive for it. That is how the one Reality creatively endures.

The first and second chapters of the Upaniṣad treated the universal creativity and the individual procreative capability as dialectical counterparts, as opposite poles a situation. The second and third stanzas of the third chapter presented the two realms of mental existence and physical existence as similar counterparts. The concluding words, 'He, with this enlightenment' indicates what the final teaching of this Upaniṣad is, what the contemplative dialectical method of approach resorted to was, and what the ultimate value of this teaching is. Attaining immortality is that experienceable ultimate Value.

शान्तिपाठः

ॐ वाङ् मे मनसि प्रतिष्ठिता, मनो मे वाचि प्रतिष्ठितमाविरावीर्म एधि; वेदस्य म आणी स्थः; श्रुतं मे मा प्रहासीरनेनाधीतेनाहोरात्रान् सन्दधामि; ऋतं वदिष्यामि, सत्यं वदिष्यामि; तन्मामवतु तद्वक्तारमवतु; अवतुमामवतु वक्तारम्।। ॐ शान्तिः शान्तिः शान्तिः।।

Glossary

Abhayam: Fearlessness. One of the aspects in which the knowledge of *Brahman* is experienced as a value.

Āditya: The sun. The god Sun.

Agni: Fire. Also the presiding deity of fire.

Agre: In the beginning.

Ānanda (ānandam): Bliss. To be understood in the context of the Good in Western philosophy as a supreme value. *Sat*, *cit*, and *ānanda* are terms conjointly used to describe the Absolute (*Brahman*) in Vedānta. Concerning an individual being, it is to be understood as the value consciousness that enables one to evaluate his own experiences either as pleasant or unpleasant.

Anna (*annam*): Food. That which could be enjoyed. Something is called *annam* because it is eaten and it eats beings. Even wisdom could be conceived as a sort of food.

Antaryāmin: The indwelling controller. Just as gold is the indwelling controller of ornaments, *ātmā* or *Brahman* is the indwelling controller of everything.

Antarikṣa: Literally, that which is perceived in the middle. The middle world conceived in the Vedas as existing between earth and heaven.

Apāna: The downward movement of vital air in an organism, especially in human body. Breathing out.

Āranyaka : A section of Vedic literature. Literally, that which is related to forests.

Arṇava: Ocean.

Ātmā (*ātman*): The self (from the root *āt* to pervade). The invisible reality or substance that pervades any visible form. Often confused with *jīva*, the soul. Used in slightly altered senses according to the context. The simplest meaning of the word is 'I' or 'oneself'.

Ātmajñāna: The knowledge of the self, self-knowledge, to know oneself.

Brāhmaṇa: A section of the Vedic literature that gives descriptive details of rituals.

Brahmajñāna: The knowledge of the Absolute.

Brahman: The Absolute. Literally, that which is always growing.

Brahmavidyā: The science of *Brahman* or the Absolute. Another name of Vedānta.

Cetana: The life principle that animates beings. *Cit* in its functional state.

Cid-vastu : (*cit* + *vastu*): *Cit* means pure unconditioned consciousness, *vastu*, substance. The one all-underlying Reality is consciousness in essence and thus is *cid-vastu*.

Cit: Literally, consciousness. The imperishable Reality pervading all the perishable and visible forms is pure consciousness in essence. Hence *Brahman* is designated as *cit*. (See *sat* and *ānanda* also).

Citta śuddhi: Purification of mind by deconditioning it. Sometimes called *sattva śuddhi*.

Dakṣiṇā: Free gifts offered to priests and *saṁnyāsins*. It is customary that priests at the conclusion of all Vedic rites, should be pleased by the sacrificer with such gifts.

Deva (*devas*): Gods. Inhabitants of Vedic heaven, meaning the effulgent ones.

Devatā: A deity. A god as understood in the context of adoration or worship. Every Vedic hymn has a deity who is praised, a *chandas* or a particular metre in which it is composed, and a *ṛṣi*, the seer who composed it.

Dik: The direction of the compass. Also means space.

Idam: This. Stands for 'this world', the world here and now.

Jāgarita: The waking state. One of the three states of consciousness. One is conscious of external objects and enjoys gross objects with senses fully functional, in this state. (see *svapna* and *suṣupti*)

Jñāni (*jñānin*): One who possesses wisdom.

Kalpam : A sacred precept or rule. In the Vedic context, the discipline which lays down the ritual and prescribes rules for ceremonial and sacrifical acts. One of the Vedāṅgas. Also the deluge.

Kalpādi : The mythological concept of the beginning of the world after a deluge (*kalpa*, deluge + *ādi*, beginning).

Kalpānta : The mythological deluge in which all specific entities attain a subtle state and merge back in utter darkness. (*kalpa* the deluge + *anta* the end).

Karma: Action. All actions are included under this term, more specially ritualistic actions.

Loka: The world. That which could be looked at.

Lokapāla : The protector of the world.

Madhyamā : The third step in the psychological process in the development of words. The stage in which a mental vision becomes conformed to a medium of expression. (See *parā*, *paśyantī* and *vaikharī*).

Mahā-vākya : Literally 'the great sentence'. Applied to the conclusive formulae of Vedāntic Wisdom, such as *tat tvam asi* (That art thou), *aham brahma asmi* (I am *Brahman*), *ayam ātmā brahma* (This self is *Brahman*), *prajñānam brahma* (Conciousness is *Brahman*), *aum tat sat* (*AUṀ*, That is what is Real), *sarvam-khalvidam brahma* (Everything here is *Brahman* indeed).

Mantra: Any stanza of Vedic hymns. Literally those words which save the person who reflects on them. Also meant to be chanted beautifully. The ritualistic part of the Vedas is also known as the *Mantra* part.

Mṛtyu: Death. The god of death.

Parā: The transcendental.

Parokṣa: Any knowledge acquired indirectly, other than through direct perception (See *pratyakṣa*).

Paśyantī: The second stage in the psychological process of formulation of words. The stage in which something definite is visualised in the otherwise clean-state-like mind (See *parā*, *madhyamā*, and *vaikharī*).

Prajñāna: Consciousness. Clean-slate-like mind.

Prāṇa: The vital breath. The functions of vital breath are identified as five, namely *prāṇa* (going upward), *apāna* (going downward), *vyāna* (that which takes vitality to every part of the body), *samāna* (that which keeps the balance of the body), and *udāna* (that which leaves the body at death).

Pṛthivī: The earth. One of the five basic physical elements.

Pratyakṣa: Direct perception. (See *parokṣa*).

Purāṇa: Literally, the ancient. The collection of legends of antiquity, meant mainly for teaching the common man, the philosophy of the Upaniṣads with the help of numerous tales.

Puruṣa : Literally, 'person'. The word is used both in universal and particular senses. In the universal sense, He is the cosmic person who has the entire cosmos for his body. In this sense He is often called *virāṭ puruṣa*.

Ṛṣi: Literally, a seer; a seer of Reality. Name applied to wise sages of ancient India who lived generally in the seclusion of forests and wrote holy scriptures of canonical importance and classical value. They were not necessarily monks, and many of them had their wives living with them. *Maharṣi* means a great *ṛṣi*.

Ṛtam: The eternal reality unfolded as the world order as well as the moral life of man.

Sādhanā: The spiritual discipline undergone for the attainment of a particular goal (*siddhi*).

Saṁsāra: The world of becoming. Literally, that which is always changing. A synonym for worldly life, considered full of sufferings.

Samaṣṭi: The universal as aganist the particular (*vyāṣṭi*).

Saṁkalpa : Mind's wilfull imagining.

Sat: That which exists always. The subsisting reality in all the transient forms of the visible world, even as gold is the subsisting reality in all ornaments. *Brahman* as this subsisting Reality is designated as *sat*. See *ānanda* and *cit* also.

Satyam : Truth or Reality metaphysically understood. See *ṛtam* also.

Suṣupti: Deep sleep state of mind.

Svapna: Dreaming state of mind.

Tapas: Austere self-discipline. Literally, 'heating up'.

Tamas: Darkness. Inert dark mode of nature.

Turīya: The fourth state of consciousness in which one gets lost in full identity with the Ultimate Reality. Defined as knowing the bottomless and topless, from top to bottom by Nārāyaṇa Guru.

Upaniṣad : Wisdom texts appended to the Vedas. Also called Vedānta as it appears at the end of the Vedas, and *jñāna-kāṇḍa* as it deals with wisdom. The word literally means 'to sit nearby and below' (*upa* = just below, *ni* = nearby, *ṣat* = to sit down). The name indicates a disciple sitting beside a *guru*. The word also means, 'the secret teaching'. The Upaniṣads teach the philosophy of *Brahman*, the Absolute. The ten major Upaniṣads are *Īśa*, *Kena*, *Kaṭha*, *Praśna*, *Muṇḍaka*, *Māṇḍūkya*, *Taittirīya*, *Aitareya*, *Chāndogya*, and *Bṛhadāraṇyaka*.

Vaikharī: The fourth and the last stage of the psychological process of formulation of words. The actual emerging of words.

Vāyu: Air. The god of air.

Vidṛti: The imaginary hole at the top of the skull.

Virāṭ-puruṣa: See *puruṣa*.

Vyaṣṭi: Any individuated or particular aspect of existence (See *samaṣṭi*).

Yajamāna: The one for whose sake a fire sacrifice is performed, who also pays for it.

Yajña: A sacrifice, sacrificial rite, any offering or oblation.

Index